legacy of EVE

WOMEN OF THE BIBLE

Nancy M. Tischler

JOHN KNOX PRESS
ATLANTA

Library of Congress Cataloging in Publication Data

Tischler, Nancy Marie Patterson.
  Legacy of Eve.

  Bibliography: p.
  1. Women in the Bible. I. Title.
BS575.T57   220.8'301'412   76-44971
ISBN 0-8042-0074-2

Contents

for—

MERLE,

ERIC,

and GRANT

Preface

At this late date, most books have been written, most ideas expressed. Solomon was surely right when he noted that, "There is nothing new under the sun." Writers have already published libraries full of commentaries on women in Scripture. Moderns have catalogued the women, traced their daily patterns of life, studied their habits of mind, and outlined the parallels among the comparative religions. They have explored marriage patterns, liturgical customs, sexuality, women's rights, and the theology of woman.

Yet perhaps some few words may still be added. The Holy Spirit speaks afresh with each reading of Scripture. Each of us is a slightly different person with a slightly different set of needs and experiences which we bring in a slightly different manner to our understanding of God's Word each time we read. Bringing new awareness of women's rights and obligations, a new openness to understanding the Scripture itself and its relevance to us, we find a thrilling freshness in the age-old stories. If we look at other women in other ages, they can show us the great diversity of God's use of women and of their response to him. In all this multiplicity, we may also discover some threads of enduring and unchanging truth.

The methodology in this book is simple: First, see what the Scripture says, (including some study of scholarly arguments on the meaning of certain words and ideas); second, consider how it is said, whether prophetically or poetically or historically; third, relate this to experience and to history; and finally, try to generalize these findings, in the context of Scripture and of human history. Usually, the study of one woman foreshadows or parallels or expands certain facets in the study of another, demanding a consideration of larger patterns. These in turn lead to the generalizations about the "images," which are the modes by which we express the universal qualities of woman.

Obviously, such a methodology is not exhaustive: The scholarship is based on secondary sources—translations rather than original manuscripts, a selection of popular critics, rabbinical scholars, church fathers, and theologians rather than an exhaustive survey. It is also personal, idiosyncratic, and limited—as is any study of controversial materials. This little book, in short, derives from thinking, reading, and writing about the roles women play. It also, necessarily, derives from my own experience of being a teacher, a literary critic, and a woman.

Because it is addressed to the common reader, male or female, it is not heavily documented except for Scripture reference. Readers should check my interpretations of Scripture against their own and argue with some of mine and with some of theirs. Any discussion of Scripture must, in the nature of things, be incomplete—neither so full nor so rich as the Scripture itself. As yet, as we all recognize, we see through a glass darkly. . . . Therefore, the book can only lead us back once more to the study of the Scripture, the searching of our own hearts, and the guidance of the Holy Spirit.

Introduction

Woman has been the favorite topic of human conversation from the beginning of time. Even when Adam chatted with God, he discussed his need for woman and his disappointment with her. Women talk about themselves and about other women; men talk about women they know or would like to know; children talk about their mothers and their sisters and their teachers.

Today in particular, woman assumes a prominent role in our casual conversations, in television shows, in news magazines, and in books. The rapid acceleration of technology has freed woman from much of her traditional role in the home. The expanding availability of products has whetted her appetite for possessions. The enlarged job market has opened up opportunities for economic freedom. The altered political scene has provided her with a vote and a place on the ballot. Her increased educational opportunities have heightened her expectations. And the feminist movement has increased her sensitivity. All of the rapid changes of the last century have come crashing down on the modern woman, producing in her an unprecedented confusion, discontent—and potential.

Faced with decisions her ancestors never needed to make, with opportunities her mother never dreamed existed, woman finds her world fraught with agony and delight. Yet she can escape only so much of the destiny determined by her biology, her social situation, and her humanity. It is consequently her difficult task to discover her own talents, her role in her society, and her relationship with other humans. Her fulfillment and her ultimate joy can result only from knowing the possibilities she can exploit and the reality she must accept.

In this search, she will find Scripture a great help, picturing as it does both the changing and the enduring aspects of human nature, speaking as it does to individual needs in all times and situations. She will discover that, rightly or wrongly, woman is now and ever has been perceived largely by means of her relationships with men (as friend, mistress, sister, wife, or mother). The single woman has almost always been the outcast, ignored or abused by an unsympathetic world. She will also discover that woman is now and always has been judged less for her own needs than for her service to others. Thus, the loyal wife, the self-sacrificing mother are generally preferred over the talented wife and the ambitious mother. Man has quite understandably lavished his praise on woman's beauty or her usefulness—those qualities which appeal to his appetites and cater to his comfort—rather than on her cleverness or her sensitivity, qualities which challenge his supremacy.

It is interesting to study Scripture with these insights, to seek new meanings in the age-old relationships, to notice those rare moments when men (or women) have looked at women as individuals, as fellow human beings with their own talents and troubles. Generally, perception is limited by one's culture and expectations. This is often apparent in Scripture, which chronicles in the history of the Jews the changing values of this mid-Eastern people. Different sections of Scripture, placed in juxtaposition, can brilliantly highlight the alteration of awareness and attitudes.

Though a perception of changing presuppositions can help us to understand our own prejudices and judge our own values, we also need the guidance of a basic doctrine of Woman—a statement of her fixed and universal being. We need to consider whether it does in fact actually differ from the doctrine of Man as stated by the church, and if so, in in what details. As Adam and Christ are usually our primary figures in determining our doctrine of Man, we must add to them Eve and Mary for determining our doctrine of Woman.

Though the role of woman has changed considerably over the past century, not even this has changed so much as our knowledge of Scripture. Discoveries by archaeologists, scientists, and linguists have enlarged, tested, and altered our perception of the Word. The continual revision of history, language, and religion, based on the deluge of new data, has forced the Christian to reconsider his own reading of Scripture. He may respond to this information explosion by becoming an ostrich, a hawk, or a chameleon—ignoring everything new, fixing hungrily on those new data which verify his own assumptions, or changing his ideas and his faith to fit each wind of doctrine in his new environment. None of these responses satisfies the Christian who respects and enjoys human knowledge, but trusts in the enduring truth of God's Word.

Some of our solution may lie in the *Word* itself—for words are not truth (though the Word is). Words are a net we use to try to catch the truth, but they are as changing and fallible as the people who write, speak, and read them. Surely we do not trust in the artifact itself—the ink, the paper, the symbols, the sounds—when we trust the Word.

A standard process of literary analysis is to note that three factors are involved in a work: the author, the artifact (or physical remains), and the audience. The human authors—the voices, accents, languages of the Scripture—are as varied as the types of literature that they wrote. Some sang their words, some preached them, some spoke them privately to God. The variety of authors, and the multiplicity of genres (or forms) were necessary to speak to a wide range of audiences, both male and female: nomadic herdsmen, farmers, housewives, warriors, slaves, kings, queens, Jews, Greeks, Romans, Babylonians, children, cripples, and religious officials. Thus, Scripture is not one book, but a whole library. It speaks in many voices, to many needs, in many manners; and it demands many responses.

As a later audience, far removed in time from those original people who could hear the words in the original language and in the original social and cultural context, we must tread a more laborious path to understanding. As we seek to grow increasingly sensitive to the clues in the artifact (in this case, Scripture), we must use any aesthetic, intellectual, or spiritual insights available to enlarge our awareness. Although we can never fully recapture the entire vision of the author, because communication is always limited by our humanity, we can and do have miraculous moments of insight. If such an aesthetic or emotional response is possible even in secular art, when the careful study of form and setting can bring a thrill of understanding, how much more can come from Scripture.

When we deal with the Bible, the author is an amenuensis for God himself, a pen in the hand of the Almighty. He has preserved the fading ink and crumbling parchment or kept the words alive in human hearts for later transcription. And the audience (each individual reader) has the Holy Spirit helping to interpret the ancient but unaging words. No wonder our response to Scripture is more than an aesthetic experience. It is a mystic unity with God, when the Word becomes flesh and dwells among us and in us.

Even for the simple, untutored Christian, who is blessed with the wisdom of God and with "ears that can hear," the words are rich with meaning. It becomes even more exciting as we bring to it some of the resources of scholarship. Still, the Christian scholar may never look coldly at Scripture as simply literature—i.e., form without faith. Nor may he look at it simply as historical artifact—a shard of the past, like a piece of old pottery which is significant only for the light it throws on human history and language. This book (or library of books) is vital and immediate in a way that forbids such fragmentation. We may dissect parts of it for the moment, but we must finally return to the entirety to test the insights of the fragment.

The evidence of Scripture on the subject of woman is scattered throughout the books. Some appears only as a few words spoken by the rabbi or narrator, some is in the form of words spoken by others about a woman, some may be the thoughts of the woman or her actual words. Some women appear only in their actions, and sometimes the evidence is the unspoken word. Many women are presented as models of proper behavior, some as warnings to future generations. Most are nameless.

In this book, we look at the more significant examples. We study them (using historic, social, archetypal, and formal approaches), we compare them to one another and trace patterns of progression or contrast. By doing all this, we hope we can finally come to understand the basis of our own beliefs. As we bring to each example the appropriate critical approach and the relevant scholarship, we should listen for the voice of God, speaking clearly and steadily throughout all the images, and we should seek the guidance of the Holy Spirit.

CHAPTER I

Eve—
the Complete Woman

It all started with Eve. Man slept through her creation and has been puzzled by woman ever since; whether she be Sarah, Delilah, Mary, Jezebel, Salome, or Deborah, she has fascinated and confused man. In this first female we can perceive hints at the many roles women were to play throughout human history. And in Adam's response to her, we can project many of the attitudes men would take toward women. In the total narrative of Genesis, we can also see what women will perceive their own true nature to be. Thus, any study of biblical doctrines of woman must start where God started—with Eve.

The story of Eve presents us with a truth about woman, her relationship to man, her dual nature, her blessings, and her curse. Scientific knowledge and scholarly study of Scripture have long been at odds with the literal acceptance of Eve's story. They quarrel about Adam's rib, about Eve's name, about parallels in other religions, about her sin, and about her nature. Even if the scientists are right in their theories of her origin, and even if the linguists are right in their insistence on the historical layers and the winnowing process of oral transmission of her story, there is still a truth in Eve. Many modern scholars, for example, insist that Genesis consists of several narratives, written at different times by different authors, much of it lost, so that only fragments remain, patched crudely together and edited by some unknown scribes. The miracle of Scripture shines through as we wonder at the possibility of multiple authorship. If Eve's message can outlive all the interpreters, all the antagonists, she must hold something of God's truth in her image.

Scholars of comparative religion note that the Hebrews' story of creation is itself unusual: It was not a sexual creation resulting from Mother Earth's union with the winds, nor a violent collision of male and female cosmic forces, nor a hatching of the World Egg. God *said,* and it was, and he saw that it was *good.* The word, the creation, the evaluation. The idea and the power brought forth the creatures, order came out of chaos, goodness out of the Word of God. And so it was with woman:

So God created man in his own image, in the image of God he created him; male and female he created them. [1]

This magnificently simple statement is rich in meaning, though stingy with specific detail. Scripture is silent on most of the questions we usually want answered: Was this one woman or was it womankind? What did she look like? Certainly she must have been physically perfect, but what would that mean in actual fact? Was she full-grown at creation? Any painter finds Eve a challenging subject, challenging him to create "perfection" as he sees it, but thwarting him by her universality. Each person has a unique notion of the ideal woman. Any sketch must perforce violate most visions and satisfy only a tiny fragment. (Even Michelangelo saw her as too heavy for most modern tastes, and too clearly neo-classical to satisfy others.) Perhaps the beauty of the words lies in their starkness, their lack of specificity. They allow each woman to see in Eve at creation an image of her own full and perfect self— sanctified. Each of us knows we have within us a potentially "good" being, if we were capable of identifying and completing it; but the world, the flesh, and the devil abort that being, distort it, and leave it twisted and incomplete. Not so with Eve: God looked at his creation and saw that it was good.

The absence of race, like other physical references, may point to a common parent for all races and to a lack of interest in such peripheral matters. It may emphasize Eve's encompassing of many stories in her own narrative. The words deal only with essence, ignoring the accidents of time, place, and individual idiosyncrasies that so often dominate our thoughts. If asked to describe a person, we most often focus on her differentiating qualities—her race, her talents, her faults, her clothing, her accent—while ignoring her essential humanity. Rather than specifying that Eve was an eighteen-year-old brunette with gorgeous figure and limited vocabulary, Scripture tells us that Eve was woman, created by God in his own image.

The very bareness of the words, *male and female created he them* provides the essence of the story. The essentially human comes first: in the image of God, as nothing else in creation. The essentially feminine comes next: differentiated from the male in her secondary characteristics, sharing with him in his humanness. No woman could ever be more liberated than Eve: free to be human, free to be feminine. History has all too often been a record of our forgetting either the humanness or the femininity.

The biblical creation story contrasts dramatically with the creation stories of other Near Eastern religions: Mankind is no mistake coming late in time, no result of stones being pitched down a mountainside. Mankind comes at the climax of creation, by design, in the image of God, differentiated sexually. Some scholars argue that this first creation story tells of Lilith, Adam's legendary first wife, who supposedly became a temptress and a witch after leaving him. Others insist that this first human creature was androgynous, necessitating surgery to divide mankind into two sexes. The more common and natural pattern is to accept this "male and female" description in Genesis as the narrative of woman's creation, not worrying about witches or hermaphrodites.

In fact, rather than insisting on adding to Scripture, we can find rich lodes by digging deeper into the words God and man have wisely preserved. The two creation narratives, left side-by-side, hold the remarkable truth within them. No myth of an earlier wife-who-turns-witch seems necessary to explain the dual presentation. Eve, whether bone or dust, shared with Adam the image of God. Her closeness to this man is expressed in a variety of ways, but always asserted as a part of her nature.

If we agree, then we may establish the impressiveness of this first woman, or these first women. For the Scripture passages before and after it imply that woman, like man, was the crowning glory of God's creation. Thus she was not simply meant to be a "higher animal." Women have been classified so often as chattel and have acted so frequently like ruminating beasts that we are pleasantly surprised when we recall that the image of God yet lurks behind the bloated face of the fishwife or the painted mask of the harlot.

Woman, like man, was created in the image of God, suggesting that God transcends male-female differentiation. She, like man, was blessed. She, like man, was given dominion over the created world. An inordinate proportion of woman's life is given over to service, often as a loving slave to families, homes, gardens, and pets. Acting as chambermaid to the dog, defeated by the unyielding weeds, woman often feels dominated by nature. Yet, in her original form, she herself had dominion.

Her femininity appears not to have made her a lesser man, who must envy man for his superiority. Rather, she herself is a separate and necessary vehicle for the fulfillment of God's injunction, *Be fruitful and multiply. . . .*[2] Her ability to conceive and bear children is part of woman's blessedness (as Mary later demonstrated), not her curse. The fecundity, meant to be a joy, has instead often became woman's tragic burden. In Eden, each new child would be a blessing, not a source of emotional and physical stress. We all know something of Eden's blessedness, but for us it is even briefer than for Eve.

And finally, God looked at Eve, as well as at Adam, noting, *And behold, it was very good.*[3] Contrary to the whole myth of the west, woman was not an evil creation. She shared with man in the primal goodness. Thus, in Eve, we see the God-created, blessed mate, potentially able to share with man in the subduing of the created world and in the propagation of the species. Her role as wife and mother are implied, though not in any limited or negative sense, in her gift of sexuality and fruitfulness. God by this means delegated to humans the capacity and the responsibility to multiply and thereby freed himself of any need for subsequent creations.

This maternal figure, Eve—"the mother of all living"—thereby became the womb from which mankind would spring. Her freedom would allow her to use her sexuality for blessing or for perversity. So far, sexuality, like nakedness, was good—innocent and pure. Neither she nor Adam would see any need for shame until after the Fall. In her potential for motherhood also lay a certain freedom: to be either the loving, nurturing mother or the hideous, devouring one. "Mother" is an ambivalent term, suggesting only the mystery of conception and birth, not the moral response to the relationships that weave their way through this recurrent miracle. Motherhood soon became a complex condition for women, an opportunity for immeasurable good or evil.

The placement of "male and female" together in this coordinate structure implies equality, and harmony: a happy balance of opposites that compose the whole of man. The Eastern idea of Yin and Yang suggests something of this union of distinct entities into a whole, a rich complementing of opposites. The resultant harmony parallels the ideal concept of marriage as a union that far exceeds the sum of its parts. Harmony appears to be part of the blessedness and goodness of this creation: Knowing only good, the couple could know nothing of strife over equal rights.

The very assertion of rights is a sign of hostility or separation. When one must undertake the task of emotional bookkeeping; when one must respond to hurt by self-assessment and self-assertion, then the relationship is already damaged. The hostility may end in exaggerated rhetoric or in genuine remorse, but the wholeness is gone. That woman must assert her rights is a sign of hurt. That she must demand action is a signal of bad faith. That man must be prodded shows his blindness or arrogance. And that he is reluctant to respond proves his selfishness or his doubt of her value. Even eager, though tardy, capitulation can seem an evidence of condescension or of guilt. In any case, the need for discussion of rights is evidence *per se* of a damaged relationship. It would be paradise indeed to have that blessed primal harmony, to have no quarrel over whether man appeared first in the listing and whether such primary placement implied favoritism. Later, Christ would point to a renewal of harmony, of true community, by noting the irrelevance of being first or last and the greater spiritual blessedness of accepting the secondary position. In a true paradise, no one would notice such order —or else each would stand aside for the other and let God make the judgment. (It is doubtful, however, that such self-effacement is the reason that the back pews in the churches generally fill up so much sooner than the front ones.)

But common sense dictates that one must precede the other in any listing and that the order need not imply precedence in value or in time. The second chapter of Genesis, however, encourages this derogatory interpretation by suggesting that there was an interval between the creation of man and of woman, and that woman was created as an afterthought. The entire time sequence is different here, and the narration is both expanded and reordered.

In cases where the words appear contradictory, we should assume that they have some deeper level of reconciliation. This Scripture is clearly no handbook for the study of evolution or a chemical analysis of human flesh. The truth lies deeper than such surface facts. We are less concerned about the time-table of creation than about the Creator and his creatures. Obviously, the preservation over the centuries (by the same folk who worshipped the one God) of both creation narratives, points to the symbolic truth in both. They could have re-ordered the telling or omitted one of the narratives; instead they chose to include both because both were of God and both told them something of the Author of Scripture and of creation.

However we choose to reconcile the differences in the accounts, we nonetheless see again that woman is created by God, again as a mate for man, again as a climax of creation. Earlier, God noted:

It is not good that the man should be alone; I will make him a helper fit for him.[4]

This passage is followed, not by the creation of woman first, but of all the animals. Among these man searches as a lonely stranger because *there was not found a helper fit for him.* Thus, woman is again presented as different from the animals. Her creation gives her the distinctive gift for communion with God and with man not shared by the animal kingdom. As a "fit helper," she serves as man's co-worker on earth, not intended for a life of idleness nor for one of mute submission. *Help* suggests some willingness, a common purpose, a unity of effort. *Fit helper* implies an equality of intellect, yet a secondary position, following man's lead.

Scripture here seems to tell us that we are social creatures not satisfied until we are together with other humans. The naturalness of marriage is further emphasized in the extraction of Adam's rib:

> *So the LORD God caused a deep sleep to fall upon the man, and while he slept took one of his ribs and closed up its place with flesh; and the rib which the LORD God had taken from the man he made into a woman and brought her to the man.*
>
> *Then the man said, "This at last is bone of my bones and flesh of my flesh; she shall be called Woman, because she was taken out of Man."*
>
> *Therefore a man leaves his father and his mother and cleaves to his wife, and they become one flesh.*[5]

Here, although the "one flesh" points back to the union suggested in Genesis 1, the separateness of the creation in time and mode point to a very different creature. She is now more specifically a secondary creation, though still God-created. Her role as wife takes precedence over her role as mother. Her closeness to man is both physical and psychological here—their mutual need draws them together.

The charming myth attributed to Aristophanes in Plato's *Symposium* tells of original humans who were round, with four arms, four legs, and two heads. As a result of their disobedience, the gods divided them, leaving them in the incomplete condition we find them today. The myth, which is fanciful and witty, echoes a truth of Scripture: We need one another to be fully human. Aristophanes describes his doomed people, spending their lives in search of their other halves, content only when complete. For him, and for most of us, the richest union would appear to be the original one—of male and female. In a fallen world, the other possible human unions become substitutes, and many are left to find completeness in so far as possible, in themselves. But Genesis reminds us that paradise involves a union of mind and body that makes of two "one flesh," possible in its fullest form only in the union of male and female.

The second telling of the creation story strikes many as belittling to woman, but a case may be made for the superiority of bone over dust as basic material. Nor does the rationale demand a secondary position —that which comes second may well be the better. (In fact, God may have been practicing with man so he could do his best work on woman!) That which comes from another need not be subservient to or dependent upon its source. (Every mother knows that her role in the child's birth does not cement the child to her nor make him subservient. Love is the real umbilical cord, not flesh.) Nor need woman lament over being created to fulfill man's need for a helper. This very need testifies to his weakness and incompleteness. Even paradise is not enough for man until it is shared with a woman.

Rather than quarrel over the comparative merits of these two expressions of the creation, as if we must choose one or the other, we do well to consider the insights that both have to offer into the nature of woman:

She is a creature of God;
Created with purpose;
Created in the image of God in her humanity and in her femininity;
Good at the time of creation;
By nature, close to man and needed by him;
Expected to help him in his work—to join in subduing the earth;
Commanded to have "dominion" over the other creatures of God;
Equipped to be a source of new life, and admonished to "be fruitful and multiply."

In Eve, we do see the complete woman: servant of God, regent over the lower creatures, helpmeet to man. When she rebels against any of these fundamentals in her nature and situation, she finds herself less than woman, less than human. Unfortunately, the story of the human race has been a series of rebellions leading to incompleteness, sloth, and perversion. Eve herself points to the path of history, showing us not only what humanity was born to be, but also what humanity chose to become.

Those golden days in Eden must have been glorious: the full joy of nature as friend, the pleasure of walking in the cool of the morning with one's mate, feeling the closeness of the flesh without any sense of shame or nastiness, enjoying the harmony of one another, the animal world, the created universe, needing no clothing nor protection nor heavy labor, speaking openly to God, without guilt or confusion. To find each day a new delight of discovery: This would be the glory of innocence. Faced with this incredible blessedness, this potential for service to God, companionship with man, and dominion over creation, Eve chose first to develop her potential for bad judgment, bad company, and rebellion.

There is clear indication that Eve, like Adam, knew God's unequivocal prohibitions. She recited them to the snake like a clever schoolgirl reciting her lessons: *We may eat of the fruit of the trees of the garden; but God said, "You shall not eat of the fruit of the tree which is in the midst of the garden, neither shall you touch it, lest you die."*[6] Then, also like a precocious but adventuresome child, she listened breathlessly to the serpent's perversity: *You will not die.* And with a child's precipitiousness, she abandoned riches for tinsel.

Her crucial choice is rich in symbolic meanings. Most commonly, men have chosen to believe that woman fell and man came tumbling after. Therefore, they insist that Eve was the mother of sin. She became for the Hebraic-Christian tradition a Pandora, who opened up the casket of evils and let them loose on the world. However, the ease with which she in turn played the serpent to Adam proves him to be as eager a sinner as she. They do indeed have twin natures. Her temptation was in some ways the one the world would consider the more masculine—*So when the woman saw that the tree was good for food, and that it was a delight to the eyes, and that the tree was to be desired to make one wise, she took of its fruit and ate. . . .* Unlike Pandora, who was merely curious and mischievous, Eve succumbed for nutrition (or gluttony), for aesthetics (or sensuous delight) and for wisdom (or cynicism). *The Interpreter's Bible* adds that her real motive was desire for power.

Perhaps in these motives, none of which was really an excuse, we may discover something of woman's (and man's) essential nature and besetting sins. Cultures have often developed woman's senses more than man's, encouraged them to be more concerned with color and shape and texture, with taste and sound. Obviously, the world is full of extremely sensitive men, including artists, musicians, and connoisseurs, who challenge this generalization. And certain cultures, especially those in the Orient, emphasize aesthetic sensitivity as a masculine quality. But women generally have given more of their lives to the gratification of the senses than have men. Cooking, sewing, weaving, decorating, arranging, mending, cleaning, and multitudes of household chores encourage women to develop a responsiveness to sensory stimuli.

If, however, we use the temptation of Eve as the means for establishing her universal and distinct characteristics, we find a problem. We are tempted to assign culturally determined traits to women as if they were secondary sex characteristics. Thus, we assume that because most American women are better cooks or decorators than their husbands, then women must have more sensitive or highly developed aesthetic equipment than men. The vast number of exceptions disprove this hasty generalization easily. And we could also document the long history of acculturation, where women have traditionally been assigned the role of gratifying the senses—cooking, sewing, weaving, decorating, arranging, mending, and cleaning. Some enjoy this work and find it fulfilling—and some do not. We find a parallel pattern among men.

If too we assign the beauty and taste elements of the temptation to Eve alone, then we must logically assign the wisdom to her exclusively as well. And most critics would be reluctant to define woman's difference from man as her appetite for wisdom and his lack of it. Certainly Eve's choice of wisdom or knowledge is an interesting one and perhaps another indication of her essential nature. She already knew good and she knew God. So she apparently chose to know evil—and as Milton said —to know good through evil. Perhaps we humans can never be satisfied with paradise until we have lost it, and we never recognize Eden until we have lived outside it. The anguish of such discovery is that we can never go back to innocence, to the pure joy of simple pleasure without the admixture of evil.

Perhaps, given the Greeks' Pandora and our Eve, this adventuresomeness of the mind is simply a natural part of women's equipment. While man may venture physically across the seas or engage in battle, woman's biology usually traps her into a more limited physical sphere with less vigorous activity. Therefore, she may well compensate by being mentally adventurous, seeking her excitement in danger and in change, even though she may thereby jeopardize her safety and peace of mind. The housewife, a prisoner of her daily chores and charges, often finds adventure in books and speculation. To break the monotony of her routine, she may seek out or succumb to temptations both mental and physical. We humans are by nature adventure-loving creatures who have a limited tolerance of peace. Like Nora of Ibsen's play, women often find the doll's house cloying. We will gamble Eden for excitement.

Of course, we must admit that Eve, in all of her choices, may be more essentially human and less specifically feminine. Her rationale may well be shared by Adam. Thus, in any effort to separate out her feminine qualities, we must be tentative, testing out hypotheses against actual cases we know as well as by the words of Scripture.

The choice made by both Adam and Eve demonstrates the paradoxical nature of human freedom: the freedom to put our will above God's. The consequence is an enthrallment to our own desires and a loss of the greater freedom of God's will. Later Dante was to picture the real freedom of the will in his *Paradiso*—"His will is our peace." Until man learns to give his will back to God, he can never know real joy. Eve and Adam, in choosing to eat of the forbidden fruit, embarked on a journey into self-will and arrived at the knowledge of evil that invariably ends such a journey. Adam is often pictured as taking the more submissive role of follower in this headstrong quest, making the unmanly excuses of love and ignorance.

Artists have been inclined to picture Eve, aware of her beauty and sensuality, enticing the innocent Adam. But he would no longer have been innocent if he responded to such a perversion of God's riches. Other commentators suggest that he ate unwittingly of the fruit she shrewdly handed him, hardly a likely explanation in the context of the Scripture narrative. Yet others romanticize his gesture, making it a weakness of human love—sacrificing paradise for love of woman.

The Scripture itself is bare of explanation: *She took of its fruit and ate; and she also gave some to her husband, and he ate.*

Scripture does not chronicle the true motive for Adam's sin, though the man insisted, *The woman whom thou gavest to be with me, she gave me fruit of the tree, and I ate.*[7] However, this self-serving protest is followed by Eve's parallel shifting of blame: *The serpent beguiled me and I ate.* Though God then cursed the serpent, he apparently took the humans' testimony with a grain of salt. If he knew they lied (at least in part), then we must follow God's lead and admit that Adam acted only partially out of love.

An act of individual sin, such as Eve's, is never a completely independent act. Sin is like a spiderweb; touch it and watch with wonder as the sticky threads lead outward in all directions. Seeking Godlike knowledge, Eve discovered that God's knowledge encompasses evil as well as good and therefore is filled with pain. Seeking the pleasure of the moment, she discovered the cost is unending and the pleasant taste soon grows bitter on the tongue.

She also found, as she sought to involve Adam, that sin is lonely. Even shared sin drives a wedge between the accomplices. The pair immediately turned on one another, now alienated from each other and from God, losing their primal harmony in the discord of mutual blame. They twisted their shared innocence into a guilty conspiracy and found themselves drawn together less by love than by loneliness and loss.

Both man and woman must bear the blame for the act of deliberate disobedience; both sinned. God's dual punishment indicated his dual judgment. He gave man travail of one sort and woman travail of another. Sex became a source of anguish—a cycle of desire, subservience, and pain—the curse woman has indeed known through the centuries. And man found his labors, his new enmity with nature, his parallel curse.

Curiously, both of these curses are but distortions of the original creation roles. Man was meant to have dominion over nature, but after the Fall, man found nature his enemy as often as his friend, and dominion no easy thing to establish. (Ask any gardener.) Woman was to be fruitful and multiply; she was created to be flesh of man's flesh. That "good" creation, distorted in her fall, confuses the beauty of her body with the shame of her nakedness. Until the Fall, her sexuality was an innocent party to their mutual delight, her nudity a source of aesthetic pleasure. After the Fall, her body became a possession to be coveted, and she learned to use man's desire as a weapon against him. The harmony was thereby converted into a veiled and recurrent war between the sexes.

The story of the Fall expands this image of woman to show us:

> In her being is a potential for evil as well as for good.
> She sins for psychological, physical, and philosophic reasons.
> She involves others in her evil.
> She tries to shift the blame.
> She turns God's blessing into woman's curse.

The literary critic is inclined to follow the archetypal approach here, seeing in Eve a universal statement of female behavior, symbolized poetically and beautifully in a single figure. The archetype is an image of the collective unconscious. Archetypal criticism is useful in religious literature because it allows the critic to use the patterns that recur in human consciousness for considering why an event or character was preserved in the people's myth. If we assume that God created us in his image, then our minds and beings must bear the imprint of his nature. Our desire for love or beauty or justice or goodness may well be an indication of our likeness to him. We hunger and thirst after him and are content only when he feeds us. This would account for the ready response humanity has to myths of the Fall or the Resurrection, even when they occur in literature outside the Judeo-Christian tradition. They echo dimly the truth that we know in Adam and Christ. Thus, one explanation of the oral tradition forming gradually over the ages the tale of Eve is that this story conforms to a deep inner need, an image which God put within generations of Hebrew people. We still select out of stories those details of plot, character, setting, or theme which speak to our universal human needs. Since God has created us and he guides us, he remains the author of our thoughts and the editor of our words when we allow ourselves to be instruments of his will. The long preservation of Eve's story in oral tradition testifies to her significance for generation after generation of Near-Easterners. As a collective statement of woman's nature and activity, she became a powerful tool for understanding woman and for justifying her position in society. Thus, poetically, psychologically, and socially, Eve was and still is of enormous significance.

Scripture indicates that Eve's life continued for years after the expulsion. One wonders what recriminating, comforting, loving, or resentful words she and Adam may have exchanged as they were pushed out of the Garden. They had their dearly purchased wisdom at last—the bitter-sweet wisdom that comes with the loss of innocence. They knew their nakedness and covered their shame. They discovered the world of evil that lies East of Eden in every man's and every woman's experience. They had one another, that thrilling completeness, but they had lost blessedness, that binding force of God's love.

These exiles from paradise shared their loss, discovered their world, settled down to their daily chores, and matured in understanding. On the sad foundation of evil and the painful expectation of death, the guilty pair built their life-in-exile together. Their children, born in pain and ignorance, were a sad reminder of that first order God gave in Eden. Now new birth became their only hedge against death and obliteration for the race, the only possible immortality for the seed of the individual. New life was man's only hope in the face of his own impending death.

The couple soon knew the pain of death—death with greater sorrow by far than any pain of birth. Their children inherited their parents' selfishness and self-will. The curious mixture of good and evil that now characterized fallen humanity made Cain jealous of his brother at the very moment he worshipped God. Eve, the mother of mankind, saw her children growing up as small and painful mirrors of their parents, mixing vivacity, deceit, shame, and desire for recognition. Needing God —but missing the closeness to him that Adam and Eve had once known, having none of their parents' primal purity, learning that punishment invariably follows sin—these children soon learned that God rules outside as well as inside Eden. They learned to worship God, a sorry substitute for the breathtaking experience of walking with him in the cool of the morning. They learned that sacrifice may in part expiate sin, but any ritual falls far short of the joyous fellowship the sinless couple had once known.

That Eve or Adam taught their children about God is apparent in Cain's and Abel's sacrifice. That the parents taught them clumsily is evidenced in their competition for God's love and in Cain's confusion about the spirit of worship. The reader suspects a parallel competition for favor in the home led Cain to expect to buy God's grace cheaply with grain from his field rather than with love from his heart. Eve discovered in time the greater pain of birth: not the travail but the separateness of will. She discovered a little of God's pain in creation—the knowledge that the child is free to do evil and to break the parent's heart. Ironically, she did come to a knowledge that she sought—the knowledge of good and evil, like the knowledge of God. In her pain, she lived through an experience parallel to God's own: the creation of new life, the recognition of its sinful nature, the loss of its fellowship. Thus she knew the fulfillment of God's prophesy, *I will greatly multiply your pain in childbearing.* [8]

We can only guess at this real or archetypal Eve's life in those days: dressed in her garments of skins, learning the rudiments of growing and preparing food, helping her husband toil to bring grain from the ground, meat from the animals, fruit from the trees, then helping Adam teach their sons to help with the work of the field and the flock. Her repeated pregnancies must have been frightening and mysterious to her, as she bore these children in solitary pain.

Woman's role has always been both innate and social. God told Eve that her biology would dominate her life, that she would "groan" in childbearing. The bearing and nurturing of children, at least until recently, have indeed dominated the lives of the mass of women. Humankind has gradually reduced the pain of birth and the burden of the nurturing role, finding ways to lessen the one and share the other. But pregnancy and childbirth remain for women either the painful interruption of a career or the blessed climax of life, even today. And though early woman may have known less of the blessedness than the burden of procreation, her childbearing must have been the central event of her comparatively brief life.

Adam and Eve must have watched with dread and love as these children grew ominously into copies of their parents, aping their sins, and giving bitter new dimensions to their Fall. Eve's sorrow must have been unbearable when she learned of Abel's death and of Cain's guilt.

Now at last she saw that she was both Mother of all Living and Mother of all Dying. The exile of Cain must have intensified the anguish still more: Her failure of love, first to God and then to Adam, found its ironic mirror in Cain's sin. The anguish she knew in her child's sin was surely intensified by the fact that his sin turned first against his brother and that it resulted in exile from his parents. Thus, by this woman's first sin and by Adam's was God's good creation turned into a world of violence, exile, dishonesty, favoritism, and death.

Such a universal tale must have echoed familiarly in the hearts of early women who learned these lines with their minds and with their lives. Cain and Abel—the herdsman and the farmer, the wanderer and the settler—were representative of a social difference reaching from the dawn of civilization. Though brothers in the flesh, their antagonistic natures and life-styles would have made them enemies in due time. Their gifts of bread and blood, the fruit of their labors with animal and vegetable life, were to become the traditional sacrifices to God, finally culminating in the great symbols of the Eucharist.

Every woman learns that her sons express their free will first in war against her and then against one another. The selfishness and possessiveness the mother knows as she hovers over the little child appears in this expanding rebellion. Certainly the primitive mother must have responded with mixed emotions at the "heroic" brutality and independence the tribe cultivated and admired in her manchild. Then as now, woman discovers that no child is truly hers for long.

In reading the Cain-Abel story, we sense a much larger meaning that lurks behind the literal fact. And we need the help of anthropologists and "myth" scholars to help us dig toward these hidden treasures. Scholars such as Robert Graves, in working with the legends of ancient peoples, have discovered that most "myths" are in fact based on historical events. Especially in the days before written records, when men passed on their wisdom orally, the telling often altered the shape of the event. Details would disappear, numbers would change, events would be telescoped. But men would transmit orally the essential core of the event, often in curiously disguised form. These stories not only chronicled the significant events of the past, but explained attitudes and formed behavior. They are therefore politico-religious history in disguise.

Among the characteristics apparent in this process of oral revision are the reduction of groups to single characters, the mixing of chronology so that stories out of different periods are merged in the telling, and the use of symbolic actions. This type of story demands imaginative reading to discover its meaning. Thus, the reader of Genesis using the "mythic" approach necessary for folk epics might consider that *Eve* may have been the singular name for a group of women who shared similar experiences and recognitions. The Cain/Abel story could easily be the simplified description of the two modes of life and worship, naturally antagonistic. They could be either a singular or a collective historical event, remembered and recorded by successions of people who witnessed the inevitable strife of human natures. Cain and Abel, brothers who battled, may have been remembered because their anger explained the psychological patterns that cause kindred tribes as well as brothers to turn violently on one another. That God could use generations of minds to shape his story and assimilate his truth is just as miraculous as his later use of a single voice to enunciate his prophecies and judgments. We invariably underestimate God's enormous versatility.

The rest of God's prophecy also followed Eve into her new life: *Your desire shall be for your husband, and he shall rule over you.* The repeated births are chronicled without reference to her role in the bearing and without names for those daughters she bore. We know the names of the sons, and we know that Adam lived eight hundred years after he became the father of Seth. We know of Adam's death, but we know nothing of Eve's. How often, even today, a woman is known by her sons and her husband. For years, daughters were not considered significant enough to number or name. And obituaries frequently sum up a woman's life by listing her husband and her children, but saying nothing about her. The record of Eve set the pattern that is still accepted by many today.

Surely Eve, like Adam, lived long, as time was measured in that day. Seth was given her to replace Abel, but no child ever really replaces another. She must have lived to see her children unite and bear children of their own. And then she died, returned to the ground, *for out of it you were taken; you are dust, and to dust you shall return.*[9] So Eve dragged out the weary years of her life, knowing toil, pain, loss, and death.

Many women were to live lives parallel to Eve's but none could have known the anguish of the tragic transformation of her unique existence. Life is sad or hard or bitter largely because we believe it to be. Contrast with former blessedness or vigor or riches can make the ordinary life seem hateful. To have been born "good," the perfect "helper" of man, to have shared with him in domination and fruitfulness, to have walked with God in the morning mists, to have known no shame or lust or anger or jealousy or guilt—this was the youth that the weary old Eve looked back on.

With these memories she must have lamented her filthy rags, her exhausted and sweaty husband, her growing brood of demanding and brawling children. She must have learned to endure the constant drudgery of feeding her family, battling hostile nature, facing hunger and fear of wild animals, and cold and heat. The dread of death must have finally eased into the tired acceptance of it. God does often relieve our fear of death by this gentle blessing of weariness with life. And finally Eve—who had been created as the triumphant climax of the universe in the image of God himself—returned without mention to the dust from which man had come.

Her legacy is a sad one: on the one hand the potential for full humanity, rich femininity—but on the other the actual achievements mixed with disobedience, dishonesty, and death. In some ways, the remainder of human history has contained a chronicle of women burdened with the loss of that image, climaxing with the redeeming love of a Savior, who recognized the beauty of the face in spite of the sin and who could and did cleanse the sin and redeem the woman. Eve's fall was tragic for her, but need not be tragic for any woman who sees Eve as the beginning, not the end of history. Eve, disobedient to God, preceding man into sin; Mary, the humble maiden, consenting to God's blessing and becoming his vessel and vehicle for the birth of Christ.

Between Eve and Mary lived a multitude of wives, mothers, queens, harlots, and faithful servants of God. In some way, each is a daughter of Eve—whose was the essential femininity—and each makes something slightly different of her legacy and her life. These women of Scripture help us to understand both Eve and Mary—and perhaps even ourselves.

Biblical Notes

1. Genesis 1:27
2. Genesis 1:28
3. Genesis 1:31
4. Genesis 2:18–20
5. Genesis 2:21–24
6. Genesis 3:2–6
7. Genesis 3:12–13
8. Genesis 3:16
9. Genesis 3:19

CHAPTER II

Sarah's Daughters—
Woman as Wife

Eve's lonely discovery of her femininity, its joys and agonies, is lost to history. Early woman—Eve and her daughters—living in their prehistoric caves and huts, discovering crafts and skills laboriously, passing on traditions to generation after generation of daughters, added bit by bit to the sum of human wisdom. Archaeologists have uncovered the bones of Stone Age people "who lived by hunting and gathering food which grew wild."* The daughters of Eve must have learned methods of butchery, of cooking and preserving meat, of stretching and sewing skins, of selecting and mixing berries and herbs and meat and grain in various combinations for tasty dishes.

It is not clear when the responsibility of cooking was assigned primarily to woman. In all probability, the role of child-bearer and nursemaid, woman's biological destiny, forced her into a somewhat more settled existence than man. Though women have occasionally appeared as hunters and warriors, the usual division of labor has meant that man hunted those things not close at hand, while woman gathered nearby seeds and prepared all food. This division is the source of the classic roles, the bread-winner and the bread-server, which obviously helped to

*G. Ernest Wright, Biblical Archaeology, p. 30.

mold our concept of woman's basic nature. The woman is vulnerable before and after child-bearing, tied to the nursing child, sometimes for years. In a society without modern birth control methods, this means she would be pregnant or nursing for most of her mature life, consequently a prisoner of the home. Man then would increasingly assume the active role, facing the outside world: foraging in it, protecting his family from it.

In time, ancient men and women apparently learned the arts of agriculture, allowing for a more settled life. Though Cain is pictured as a grower of cereal, Noah is the one whom tradition has settled on as the first farmer. (In actual fact, it may have been a woman, confined to home, who spilled some seeds, saw them sprout, and domesticated grain.) They learned to grow cereals and grind them, to mix the flour with other products of their animals and their land. They learned that honey and salt are useful and plentiful, that they could make butter and cheese from milk, that grapes were good for juice and for wine. Edith Deen records an impressive list of foods mentioned in Scripture that apparently were used by Old Testament peoples: apricots, apples, pomegranates, dates, olives, almonds, honey, wine, the meat of goats and sheep, pumpkins, cucumbers, melons, greens, and both meat and by-products of pigeons, antelope, gazelles, and hens. Seasonings included leek, garlic, onion, sugarcane, and dill.* As contact with other peoples increased, the range of foods expanded.

Scripture tells us little of daily life in the mist-shrouded days before the Flood. All we actually know is what archaeologists confirm—that humanity increased in number. The hunting, gathering, cleaning, and cooking were invariably omitted from such records. These obvious and inevitable daily human events are not the scene of God's miraculous intervention. History records only the spectacular events or the broad summaries. Like the creation stories, the Flood left a monumental mark on human memory. The details of individual behavior and daily ritual pale before the epic proportions of this great drama of destruction and preservation. Mythic events, such as Eden or Babel, do not lend themselves to historic criticism. They are the watersheds of human history preserved symbolically in collective memory. The record preserves our species' assimilation of those moments which left ineradicable scars on

*Edith Deen, The Bible's Legacy for Womanhood, p. 41.

the human psyche, altering our view of self and of existence.

In this second judgment, a result of humanity's renewed and remarkable genius for evil, woman plays only a minor role. *The LORD saw that the wickedness of man was great in the earth, and that every imagination . . . was only evil continually.* [1] The difference between male and female evil apparently diminished before the monumental judgment on mankind collectively. Nor were women marked specifically for salvation because of their virtues; only the good *men* were chosen— Noah and his sons. Their women are noted only as "wives"—necessary for procreation, but nameless and lacklustre. The females were preserved in equal number with the males, not because they deserved salvation, but because they were necessary to God's plan. Before this angers us, we must recall that the Christian learns that not even Noah deserved salvation. And, the man who recorded God's Word, though divinely inspired, was limited by his experience in, and understanding of the world through the Hebrew culture. Yet God's grace, not merit, is the key to salvation for us all.

Medieval legend expanded imaginatively on this exclusion of reference to women's role in and response to the Flood by suggesting that Noah's wife actually attacked the ark project as visionary and impractical. When the time came for boarding (according to English mystery plays), this quarrelsome shrew resisted her God-fearing husband. She was dragged kicking and screaming aboard the ark, saved from her watery grave by her wise and worshipful husband.

When God established his post-deluvian covenant, he again omitted reference to females, perhaps less a commentary on God's view of the comparative unworthiness of the female than on his writer's use of generic reference. (Only recently have we assumed that *Man* means only man, not woman.) Regardless, woman has not found herself excluded from God's covenant. In some cases she has, in fact, been the instrument of his will. In the long run, man has treated woman with considerably more disdain than has God, and the long history of her abuse has been man's parody of God's Word. Our evidence lies in the life and teachings of Christ, which set the record straight on God's love of women as well as men.

Any woman might well justify Noah's wife's supposed obstinancy by speculating that no sane housewife would welcome her role in such a cruise. It would be by any measurements the archetypal housewife's nightmare.

Certainly housekeeping even on dry land could have been no easy task for early wives. Whether in caves or in tents, where many of these nomadic people would have lived, and later in tiny huts, they would have known gruelling lives. Without artificial light, except from fire and later oil lamps, the wife must have gauged her days by the sun: rising, working, and resting by its light. Scripture mentions the cool of the morning, a pleasant time in most warm climates. The heat of the midday sun must have driven her inside to rest and to work under shelter. The late hours became a time to go to the well for water and perhaps to gossip with others. Washing clothes was apparently communal as well, but water was so scarce that only in the later days of the kingdom do we find references to bathing at home, and even then the custom apparently was not common for women of a rank lower than Bathsheba's. Water was so precious that the sharing of water at the well was seen as a gracious gesture, even so late as Jesus' day.

Most women probably spent much of their days as now, in preparing food for their families. They learned to bake in clay pots with removable lids, heated by hot stones; they learned to extract oil from the olives for a variety of uses, to mix water or milk with flour and leave it for sourdough yeast, to churn butter, to store the abundance of the harvest against the barren seasons. The large variety of storage urns points to pantries stocked with grain, oil, wine, dried herbs, and other valuables. The women served their large families out of large bowls, shared by the entire group which dipped into them. The family sat on straw mats or on the grass, and the dishes were placed on the floor.

For recreating the daily life, the utensils, the food, the activities of these ancient peoples, archaeologists are invaluable. Fragments of history set our imaginations awhirl in picturing the clothing, the homes, the daily habits of those early people. Scripture, recording the spiritual ebb and flow of human life, seldom feeds our hunger for details of physical activity. Our own lives are so taken up with concern for diet, dress, and housing that it is instructive to see that these are the very details omitted when chronicling the essentials of human history. By having her life so firmly fixed on these tedious minutiae, woman has often stepped out of the center stage of history, cooking the stew while the men plotted the battle, sweeping the floor while the men preached the words of salvation.

Although Ruth, one of the rare women in the forefront of God's covenant people, shows us that later on some women could work in the fields, the gleaners were clearly seen as poverty cases. Tending the herds was considered dangerous work and therefore usually delegated to men, while women were kept in the more protected environment of the home.

As time went on, women apparently had increasing freedom to move through the larger environment of the town or the city. When Lemuel (or Solomon) pictured the ideal wife of Proverbs, he described her day as busy and far-ranging. She rose before the sun, wandering some distance to find food for her household. Pictured as a businesswoman of some competence, she supervised a group of maidens who worked in the home, negotiated the purchase and planting of a vineyard, bought and finished wool and flax in a small home industry, and earned money for her family by her labors. The pride with which proverbial wisdom noted the good woman clothing her family in scarlet and in fine linen hints at the concerns for the average woman. Spinning the yarn and weaving the cloth to make the most simple garments must have consumed enormous time and labor. The gathering of the materials, the work at the distaff and the spindle, the dyeing of the yarn, the weaving and the sewing must have been constant, monotonous work, relieved perhaps by communal gatherings. The woman's task would have been furnishing not only the clothing of her family but the carpets, beds, floor coverings, quilts, goathair coverlets, and straw mats as well.

Gradually, specialists may have made the sandals and other leather goods for the family, but these specialists (like Priscilla) may have been women. Potters may have been women as well, but the usual scriptural reference to potters is masculine. Certainly women must have suggested the specifications, determining their size and shape and decoration by their use. Women undoubtedly enjoyed the fruits of jewelry-making crafts, perhaps even joining in some of the work. Archaeologists have found numerous brooches, combs, rings, earrings, necklaces, and nose rings that attest to love of precious stones and metals for decoration. We do know that some women wove baskets, as evidenced by the well wrought basket-boat in which Moses was placed.

With the average of seven children to each small household, the wooden cradle hanging from the roofbeams would usually have been full, and no archaeologist needs to document the constant attention necessary for the growing family. Taking care of children in nomadic days must have been, in the main, much simpler than today. There would have been no question of elaborate furnishings, piles of clothing, constant washing, or educational toys. The child would have entered a world of dirt and work and animals. If he or she survived infancy, the youngster would have grown without schools or churches or organizations. The family was all of society, the distance within seeing and walking was the universe. The child learned to worship at a rude stone altar, getting an education at parents' and grandparents' feet. The boy would have taken his place in the labor force very early, joining in the hunting of animals, the minding of sheep and goats. The maidens would have gathered around their mother in the strongly differentiated work of the female, learning their responsibilities as wives and training themselves for their work.

Even today, life is circumscribed for most children. They learn their culture, their habits, their speech, and their religion from a handful of friends and neighbors. Their world is the farm or the neighborhood, the school, the stores, and the church. Though the media tell them of a larger, more varied world outside, the parents bear the responsibility for exposing their children to those patterns they deem most valuable and cultivating the habits of life they consider essential.

The rhythm of a woman's life must have been governed by both culture and nature: the seasons, the time of day, the harvests, and her own body. The whole structure of her society and her psychology must have encouraged her to accept her role within the family, and her subservience to the boys who might become the political, religious, and military leaders. If God told her brother or father or husband to leave his country and migrate to another, she undoubtedly admired Sarai for her wise acquiescence and abhorred Lot's wife for her foolish reluctance. If her brother or husband ordered her to remain silent, she was expected to follow Sarai's example and obey. Fathers apparently arranged their daughters' marriages and, if Laban was typical, saw the daughters as their property—along with oxen and asses. Lot offered the men of Sodom his virgin daughters for their pleasure when the mob threatened his angelic visitors, demonstrating that even the virginity of the daughters was seen to be at the disposal of the father. The constant listing of women along with property suggests that they were considered chattel and must have considered themselves as such.

Yet for all this careful programming in submissiveness, the actual women remembered through Scripture were not simple ruminating beasts. Many moderns insist on the importance of environment, the limitations established by early conditioning and poor self-image. But history abundantly demonstrates the human's capacity for violating expectation and transcending limitations. God knows the potential in each of us and can fan it into flame when he so chooses. History is in part a record of the exceptional people he has chosen to contradict probabilities.

Sarai was by no means subdued in her submission—she laughed even at God. Her beauty may have set her apart as beauty so often grants privileges to its holder, but her power apparently transcended that bestowed by appearance alone. She is constantly referred to by name (an unusual honor for a biblical woman). God's special protection of her brought fear into the hearts of kings, and she knew how to dominate her regal mate. Certainly, no one could insist that Sarai was a broken spirit. She shared Abram's concern for his seed, and accepted her barrenness as God's curse. *Behold now,* said she to Abram, *the LORD has prevented me from bearing children; go in to my maid; it may be that I shall obtain children by her.* [2] The old custom strikes this modern as remarkably liberated. Few women today would share Sarai's willingness to accept her barrenness and to adopt another's child sired by her own husband, even, in fact, to arrange their intercourse. Sarai may not have been so willing, though, had it not been for the importance of male offspring in patriarchal society.

The subsequent rivalry between Abram's bedmates is, however, eloquent testimony to the unchanging nature of humanity. Hagar became arrogant with her mistress when she conceived by Abram, triggering Sarai's jealousy, hurt, and anger. And Abram's servile acquiescence to Sarai's whims suggests that human relations have ever been complex and unpredictable. Here was a rich man, the leader of his clan, a staunch man of God, who said humbly to his furious wife, *Behold, your maid is in your power; do to her as you please.* And it follows as the night the day, *Then Sarai dealt harshly with her, and she fled from her.* [3]

Genesis had early noted that woman would desire her husband. History testifies to woman's attraction to man. Even though she is often pictured as a disinterested participant in sexual activity, woman is often as enthusiastic, loving, and possessive as man. Even in arranged marriages, which to our alien view seem disastrous to affection, the marriage apparently was often happy, the couple compatible. Human nature does not really vary to any great extent. Close contact, whether in our system of single or sequential marriages, or in the older system of polygamy, breeds strong feelings, rivalries, deep commitments—as well as children. Modern views of romantic love were not a part of primitive thought, but the relations of Abram and Sarai do ring of romance and love and complex camaraderie.

There is certainly ample evidence that the wives and the concubines of the patriarchs and kings had strong disagreements among themselves. The husband invariably had one favorite, whose sons he honored above the others'. The hostility shown between the fecund Leah and the beloved Rachel would have been even more strident when the wives were not also sisters, though being sisters brings still another form of rivalry into play. Yet Sarai's very willingness to undertake the ill fated genetic experiment with Hagar suggests an openness to sexual ideas and a naivete about their consequences that gradually diminished with increasingly settled, civilized existence.

Concern for the continuance of the family line seems to be stronger in the older cultures than in ours. To Abram and Sarai, the continuance of Abram's seed was more important than their marriage. The encouragement to use Hagar as breeding stock strikes us as crude, but it recurs among the maidservants of Jacob's wives. Leah-the-unloved must, in fact, have seen herself in these terms.

If woman's only important role is as breeder, then her only crucial choice in life is the choice of the sexual mate and only her childbearing years are worth living. An incredible number of men and women still believe this travesty of human fulfillment even today. Nonetheless, barren old Sarah, at 90, still struck the loving old Abraham as more valuable than the fertile young Hagar. This preference indicates that these two old friends and lovers placed some values above simple continuation of the physical line.

After Hagar had her child, Sarah found herself also in the path of blessing, amazed that God had planned better than she. The domestic scene which preceded God's announcement suggests that Abraham had reestablished his authority in the household. After he had obtained God's blessing for Ishmael (Hagar's son), he had angelic visitors. He ordered the bringing of water to wash their feet while he hastened into the tent where Sarah waited like a dutiful wife. *Make ready quickly three measures of fine meal, knead it, and make cakes,* he ordered.[4] While she worked on the bread, a servant killed a calf "tender and good" and hastened to prepare it. And Abraham himself took the curds and milk to the visitors and served them. The scene demonstrates the hospitality of the desert, as well as the solemn ritual of etiquette, the clearly defined sex roles, and the division of labor among the ancients. It also indicates that Sarah had the manners to appear an obedient and humble wife before visitors, while Abraham assumed the role of rich and gracious patriarch. Most families, even today, appear very different in public from their private reality.

Yet even here, Sarah's strong will and independent spirit showed themselves. Apparently, Abraham, treating his wife like a harem girl, did not think to show her to the visitors and left her in the tent chafing with curiosity while they ate their hot brown bread and roasted meat. The cloistered life may have been the only life that a decent woman could live, and her husband may have been protecting her from strange eyes. But she listened to the conversation from behind the tent door, and when they told Abraham—not Sarah—that she would bear a child the following spring, Sarah forgot herself and burst out laughing. She knew that she had long since passed menopause and that a man of a hundred years has little pleasure in a woman of ninety. Yet when caught laughing, she faced it out before the guests and denied the truth. The child of her old age soon came to put a stop to her cynical laughter and to prove that nothing is impossible for God.

Motherhood must have tamed Sarah, for we hear little more of her as Isaac grew up, was threatened with sacrifice, escaped, and matured into manhood. We do not know whether she shared in this great struggle. She, like so many women, was remembered primarily for her son, not for herself. Her jealousy of Hagar did not disappear; it was transformed into a jealousy of Ishmael's love of Isaac and his share with Isaac in Abraham's estate.

Here is a case where the omissions and the focus—the very selection of incident and detail and their ordering—tell us much about the culture. While Sarah's rich individualism flashes out in her anger, her curiosity, her jealousy, or her irrepressible humor, the narrative limits her portrait. She is seen as she travels with her husband, retains her purity, conceives and bears a child. She is not included in the angelic conversation or the substitutionary sacrifice. Like Noah's wife, she appears to be a necessary adjunct to man for procreation, not a main actor in the drama of redemption.

The last poignant references to Sarah are the recording of her death (at 127 years) at Hebron, and of Abraham's great sorrow. *Abraham went in to mourn for Sarah and to weep for her.* [5] So long together, so many perils and adventures, so many arguments and reconciliations had come to an end. Abraham stood at last as a lonely old man, seeking only a burial field for Sarah and himself and a wife for their son Isaac from among their own people, a wife who like Sarah would be "willing to follow." The long marriage of Abraham and Sarah followed no simple formula. It was a rich human relationship, which involved conspiring, bending, ordering, begging, obeying, laughing, and loving. Abraham had other wives and concubines, but was buried at last beside his beloved Sarah.

The wives of the patriarchs, like the patriarchs themselves, are all of one family, but are strikingly individualized. With Rebekah, we see the courtship that we missed in Sarah's story and can guess at the standards by which the prospective bride was judged. Courtship is always a fascinating ritual dance preliminary to mating. In it, both the selection and the attraction are important and the tastes of different cultures can vary enormously. In Minoan culture, the fragile, wasp-waisted, wide-hipped, long-haired girl was the beauty. States from Mycenaen culture testify to a taste for broader lines, heavier proportions. Even today, one culture (or person) will prefer the dark, voluptuous girl, another the slender blonde. Luckily for all of us, beauty is in the eye of the beholder. When a group of people agree on a woman's beauty, then she wins the contest. But all of us realize too that an inner beauty can transform our response to physical features, softening the image and erasing the flaws. Attraction depends on compatible values and natures, not simply physical appearance. And the permanence and happiness of a marriage must derive from even deeper correspondencies of spirit.

The task of the society is to construct courtship patterns which can control the attraction while testing for lasting values. Since the survival of the species depends on good selections, this becomes a significant part of cultures. Certainly Scripture from Genesis through Revelation emphasizes the importance of the bride, finally turning her into a symbol for the church. Among the patriarchs, not individual whim but the careful choices by the family determined the appropriate wife for the son who would carry the tradition. The woman must have certain family, certain traits of character and appearance; she was screened by the trusted family servant, who invoked and received God's help, and she was judged by her actions.

Rebekah came with the other women of the city to the well *at the time of evening, the time when women go out to draw water.* She bore her water jar on her shoulder, and she was *very fair to look upon.*[6] Her innocence, directness, efficiency, hospitality, graciousness, and beauty immediately convinced the servant (on his master's behalf) to propose to her. He then presented her with a ring for her nose and bracelets for her arms (probably a portion of the bride price paid by the groom). Running home with the impetuous delight of a maiden with her new finery, she showed her mother's household and her brother Laban these new acquisitions.

These references indicate that Rebekah and Laban, like Abraham and Sarah, came from a matrilineal state (her mother's household), where the brothers (Laban) bore a special relationship to sisters. Yet for all the importance of these women's family position, Laban had the final determination in his sister's and later his daughters' marriage contracts. Laban, not Rebekah, agreed on the terms by which she would be wed.

Rebekah also reveals to us clothing customs of the age. The references to jewelry of gold and silver and the costly raiment (which were omitted in discussions of Sarah) perhaps point to Rebekah's greater acquisitiveness, though not to her greater beauty. One suspects her beauty is simply the freshness of youth, not comparable to Sarah's aging majesty. In full splendor, Rebekah rose with her maids, mounted her camel, and followed this servant to a land she had never seen and a forty-year-old man she had never met. Here we see the arranged marriage where the girl's attractiveness is mentioned as her value and the man's family and wealth as his. He apparently buys her willingness; she accepts her brother's choice eagerly. The portrait hints at an adolescent bride, vivacious, lovely, and strong, eager to leave home, to marry, to enjoy prestige and wealth. Her considerations are hardly peculiar to Rebekah, but they do not promise a happy marriage. Scripture notes that when he saw her, Isaac loved her. It does not record her feelings about him.

From here on, Rebekah's story echoes bits of both Sarah's and Eve's: the barren womb, the prayer for children, the two sons, their enmity, and her loss. The favoritism for Jacob over his twin brother might well have been her feminine preference for refinement over ruggedness. She loved Jacob, the quiet dweller in tents, rather than the hairy Esau, the skillful hunter. Since we have so little record of her relationship with Isaac, we are inclined to picture her as an unhappy wife who found her fulfillment in her favorite son. The open favoritism smacks of years of unpleasantness. The hostility toward the rough but kindly Esau may have been a result of his frivolous treatment of his treasured position, or it may have been related to Isaac's love of him. She may have been protecting the gentle, yet more guileful son, or perhaps the aging beauty found perverse pleasure in undermining Isaac's plans.

Rather than arguing face-to-face with him as the forthright Sarah would have done with Abraham, she plotted her shrewd deception and convinced Jacob to join with her in trickery (though he seems to have inherited a native inclination in that direction which his mother easily encouraged). Isaac accepted the outcome of their plot with fatality and never even (as recorded in Scripture, at any rate) accused Rebekah, though he must have recognized her devious mind in the trick and her hand in the stew.

In some ways, the failure to confront, to argue, to accuse is more painful for the guilty party than the cataclysmic recognition scene that explodes and then clears the air. She found, as we all do, that even the unproven sin exacts its toll on our lives. Her sin, like Eve's, resulted not only in her deeper estrangement from Esau and Isaac, but also in the loss of her beloved son, Jacob. Perhaps Jacob's exile made him a man; he undoubtedly needed to be away from his mother's influence. The exile certainly provided him with experience, travel, allowing him to mature in the Lord, not to mention his growth in terms of wives, family, and livestock. But the breach in the family must have been painful for Rebekah; the blind old husband dying, still angry or hurt with her, the simple Esau puzzled at her malice, and her favorite, Jacob, exiled.

Rebekah, like Sarah, found beauty both a blessing and a threat. While it brought to her a wealthy husband, who would love her at least in part for her appearance, it meant that she too tempted other men and caused some peril to the family. She too was protected by a jealous God rather than a jealous or honest husband. She too found that other women in the home (Esau's wives) "made life bitter."

Rebekah continues to remind us of Sarah, listening in surreptitiously to men's conversations, thereby acknowledging that a woman had no right to participate in man's business, even when it dealt with the most important elements in her own life, her pregnancy or her children. Even today some conversation is considered "man talk"— inappropriate for delicate female ears. Though the ladies are no longer expected to retire discreetly from the table while the men settle down to cigars, brandy, and serious or obscene conversation, there remains a tendency towards separation by sexes. Men are often expected to take care of money, of legal transactions, of business. Women are frequently expected to be content with elevating discussions of diapers, refrigerators, and recipes. This exclusion of women from serious conversation, which has reinforced their subordinate and often childlike position, is finally crumbling. But the unconscious cruelty of the custom has led many women to sneak around eavesdropping.

Rebekah's use of her stolen information shows that she was a deceptive and materialistic woman, encouraging her son in the same unscrupulous behavior. When later she caught the gossip of Esau's murder plot, she quickly planned Jacob's escape without apparent concern for her own safety. It is doubtful that this signals any new dimensions of self-sacrifice in her character; she knew Esau's good will and quick temper, she made no confession of her own complicity, and she feared neither his wrath nor his curse. She apparently knew full well that he would soon soften toward her and would in time come to love his brother again.

In such moments we perceive a shrewd, manipulating woman, who planned her son's fortunes, his escape, and his life. Perhaps like Sarah, she felt isolated among these alien women who made her life so miserable. Like Abraham, she preferred to see her son married to one of her own tribe, a girl who could share her values. Their common concern with tribe may be a matter of language, dress, traditions, and culture, not to mention religion.

Without doubt, she and Sarah shared habits of mind: independence of spirit, shrewdness, awareness of their physical beauty, and adventuresomeness. It was they, of all the women whom their husbands knew, that they cherished; it was their sons who inherited the blessing and the property. They, of all of the daughters of Eve, stand out even today as individuals, not as mythic earth mothers or as temptresses for frail humanity. Sarah and Rebekah, for all their common heritage, were nonetheless very different women. Sarai went on the God-bidden jour-

ney with her comrade-husband, undertaking the hardships of the nomadic life with him, agreeing to his strange deceits, urging him to
decisions, sharing his adventure with God while accepting grudgingly
the secondary position. No word is recorded about Sarah's views regarding the sacrifice of Isaac, probably because this was a matter strictly
between Abraham and his God. When Abraham and Sarah had a
quarrel, it was open and honest. They knew pain and they knew joy and
apparently they knew how ludicrous they appeared with their white hair
and new-born son. In their long marriage one senses a thrilling union
of male and female. It is a moving testimony to their love that, when
Sarah died at one hundred and twenty-seven, Abraham *went in to
mourn for Sarah and to weep for her.*[5]

Rebekah had no such memorial in the loving memory of her husband. She probably outlived the enraged or disillusioned old Isaac. Her
life was a striking contrast to Sarah's, perhaps because it was a later and
more settled time with fewer challenges to be a pioneer of faith and to
be a helpmeet to man. Marriage to an older man, a stranger, who wooed
her with his wealth by proxy; life among his servants as a stranger, lonely,
jealous, and conniving—these are the marks of an unhappy woman
whose climactic trick revealed greater love for her son's wealth than for
her marriage or her integrity. The pretty young bride had become the
money-grubbing trickster, using her womanly insights into the old man's
tastes and weaknesses. While Sarah argued with Abraham, Rebekah
tricked Isaac, inaugurating (at least for the record) the sly battle-plan
usually ascribed to women. The method may have been the outgrowth
of a series of limitations that women had to maneuver to avoid. It may
have been that Rebekah's world was more structured than Sarah's, that
the easy intercourse among the sexes was disappearing with wealth and
order. Or it may have been that Rebekah was a more devious and
materialistic person than Sarah. Perhaps the more settled world of Rebekah had fewer rights and less respect, with woman seen more clearly as
chattel; or perhaps Isaac was a less open and comradely husband than
Abraham. We do miss the earlier couple's conversations and sense of
openness. It is ironic that the chronicle of the romantic courtship was
followed by the deceitful marriage, and we can only speculate as to
whether custom, age, wealth, or character caused the increasing but
apparently unspoken hostility.

Their kinswoman Rachel's story is a more romantic one than either

Sarah's or Rebekah's. The abrupt meeting of the fleeing Jacob with his stranger-kinsmen at "high-day," the recognition scene at the well, the kiss and weeping in joy all testify to a more emotional, more personal attraction. The reunion of the family, the eagerness of Rachel, the jubilance of Jacob all paint a romantic picture of idyllic love, which is soon corrupted by the classic villain, Laban. The trick by which Laban foists off on Jacob the older, weak-eyed Leah rather than the young, beautiful Rachel (an ironic echo of the earlier trick also involving weak eyes, mistaken identity, and improper rewards) is but a romantic delay that heightens their suspense and their love. (Medieval love literature is frequently based on the theory that love delayed is love increased.) The reader pities poor Leah—the unlovely and unloved mate with no stature; beauty then as now took precedence and determined value. Leah bore the children and probably the blame for Laban's ruse while Rachel won the love. Thus in time, the rejected Leah bore son after son, hoping with each new baby to win Jacob's love. Instead she won her sister's envy and precipitated a quarrel between Rachel and Jacob. Even the beautiful woman was not considered complete until she bore a son. Rachel, like Sarah, provided her husband a hand-maid to serve as an alternate womb to her own barren one, but like Sarah, she found the substitute-mother arrangement less than satisfying. The sisters' competition extended to ridiculous extremes before Rachel finally bore Joseph, bringing some remission to her antagonism. The enmity between the sisters, sowed and encouraged by others, bore bitter fruit in the children, in Joseph's hostile relationship with his brothers.

For the most part Rachel seemed less wily than Sarah or Rebekah; but she did bargain with her sister, steal her father's household gods, and trick Laban and her husband by sitting on the stolen goods, pitifully and cynically pleading "the way of women" while the men searched for the idols she concealed. Yet in this, she proved herself a proper mate for the crafty Jacob. The trickster is much admired in Hebrew tradition. The female trickster—Rebekah, Rachel, even Miriam—is respected for her ability to pull off the trick and admired beyond reason if the trick is in accord with God's will. But while the male is punished for his disobedience or his dishonesty, the female is ignored. Rebekah received no recorded rebuke nor did Rachel. As if naughty children were caught in their disobedience, these women had no punishment for their sins, except that which they brought on themselves.

These women point to the man-centered values of the patriarchal culture: Their premarital chastity is the assurance that they are clean and unused vessels to receive and nurture the seed of their owner-husbands. (The tragic story of Dinah indicates that this chastity is a matter of family honor, and that one may dishonor a man by raping his daughters or sisters. Lot's offering his daughters to the angry mob, however, seems to place the honor accorded to guests above even the honor of the family in their scale of values.) Women's beauty made them more desirable possessions. Their graciousness to guests insured respect for the man's household. And their ability to bear sons provided continuation of the family line. Thus were women consistently seen as possessions, to be listed with the sheep and camels, to be protected as significant portions of a man's fortune.

Yet lingering behind these accepted values is the image of women who were fully human: clever, underhanded, arrogant, jealous, frightened, lonely, and loving. Perhaps Jacob did see Rachel as chattel (though one seldom kisses a cow in enthusiastic greeting). Yet possession or not, Rachel's death in childbirth brought real anguish to Jacob. And years later he told their son Joseph about the great sadness he felt when he buried his beloved Rachel near Bethlehem.

Solomon, who had more than his fair share of wives and concubines, described the beauty of the ideal bride in his marriage song. Tradition has also ascribed (probably falsely) the words of Proverbs to this experienced old husband. The folk wisdom of the Hebrew people, compiled poetically in this remarkable book, describes the flaws and virtues of the wives from the husbands' viewpoint. Their shrill voices and continual nagging appear to run a close second to infidelity as their greatest irritant. *It is better to live in a corner of the housetop,* asserts the wiseman, *than in a house shared with a contentious woman.*[7] Proverbs records a much later, more settled era than we have studied in the nomadic patriarchs, but in the descriptions of the good wife, we see a timeless Hebrew ideal:[8]

> *A good wife who can find?*
> *She is far more precious than jewels.*
> *The heart of her husband trusts in her,*
> *and he will have no lack of gain.*

Notice that her worth is largely financial and social. Though the maiden is coveted for her beauty, the wife is treasured for her productivity:

She does him good, and not harm,
all the days of her life.
She seeks wool and flax,
and works with willing hands.
She is like the ships of the merchant,
she brings her food from afar.
She rises while it is yet night
and provides food for her household
and tasks for her maidens.
She considers a field and buys it;
with the fruit of her hands she plants a vineyard.
She girds her loins with strength and makes her arms strong.
She perceives that her merchandise is profitable.

This description of the mature woman presents a strong, practical, businesslike person, planning her day and earning her keep. The Hebrew never seems to have any real enthusiasm for weakness or frivolity. Even in these later days of the kingdom, the virtues of the frontier survive, though modified. Apparently there was no stigma attached to women working at certain chores or transacting business; perhaps this also means that the Hebrew woman was allowed to participate in men's conversations. Although this masculine activity seems not to have interfered with her wifely virtues, the reader must modify his amazement at this competent housewife with the recognition that Solomon also had his harem, as did other kings of later days. Changes were nonetheless apparent in attitudes; though the busy housewife of Proverbs was no career woman, she was clearly no mindless beast either. Here we see her enthusiastically praised as helpmeet, working efficiently at those chores related to the welfare of her family:

Her lamp does not go out at night.
She puts her hands to the distaff,
and her hands hold the spindle.
She opens her hand to the poor,
and reaches out her hands to the needy.
She is not afraid of snow for her household,
for all her household are clothed in scarlet.
She makes herself coverings;
her clothing is fine linen and purple.

> *Her husband is known in the gates,*
> *when he sits among the elders of the land.*

Men are still the designated rulers of the city, and her work is a tribute to the good taste of her husband. While he sits with the elders, she makes and sells linen garments, in her little household industry, and *delivers girdles to the merchant.* Though these activities bring in money —the commodity that marks the later period of this selection—they are all extensions of traditional women's work. Nonetheless, her industry makes her mistress of her household (her maidens) and her money (which she earns from the merchants and shares with the poor). Her concern is first for her own family, as is her husband's, but she is beginning to move out of the sheltering prison of the home.

This woman is admirable in still another way. She is not noted for her youth, her family, or her physical beauty, but for her character: her strength, dignity, wisdom, and diligence. This vein of iron so often apparent in mature people who have been tested by life, hard work, and pain, becomes the real treasure lurking beneath the veil of appearance:

> *Strength and dignity are her clothing,*
> *and she laughs at the time to come.*
> *She opens her mouth with wisdom,*
> *and the teaching of kindness is on her tongue.*
> *She looks well to the ways of her household,*
> *and does not eat the bread of idleness.*
> *Her children rise up and call her blessed;*
> *her husband also, and he praises her:*
> *"Many women have done excellently,*
> *but you surpass them all."*

The wisdom of Proverbs interests us in a slightly different manner from the history of Genesis. Genesis is the tale of a people's beginnings, dimly recalled, summarizing through action the valued character traits and cultural habits. Proverbs is a summary of accepted values separated from individual instances or historical circumstances. Books like Proverbs appear in many people's literature, the accumulated wisdom of the ages. Their pithy and poetic phrasing makes them memorable; their quiet and generalized tone give them authority. While Genesis can show us the growth of certain emerging and unformulated attitudes, Proverbs

can help us to understand the more generally expressed and widely
accepted values. Given their difference in time and circumstance, it is
not peculiar that the images of the women are somewhat contradictory.
Certainly woman's role had changed with the more settled society and
the changing needs.

The women of Genesis picture for us a summary of what a woman's
life must have been: her youth spent in preparation for and anticipation
of marriage, her maturity spent in bearing and raising children, her old
age dedicated to living vicariously through her children. Women lived
largely through men, be they brothers, father, husband, or sons. A
woman's value to her society, and very probably to herself, lay in her
ability to attract, to please, to bear, to transmit. She was a vessel to be
formed, owned, filled, and emptied. When women dared to interrupt,
to advise, or to trick men, they were rebels against man and God. Their
role was primarily one of submission, yet we suspect they knew some
happiness and considerable love. We are too often inclined to assume
that ours is the only formula for life. A liberated woman may see the
submissive housewife as thwarted and miserable, living a life of quiet
desperation. The housewife is often equally blind to the pleasure many
women find in careers. In fact, most of us can find great joy in the work
at hand if it is our work and if we know nothing different. Even today,
many a woman washes her clothes in a river and sweeps her dirt floors
with branches. For other women, in a more industrialized society, the
accepted drudgery and circumscribed life may include a subway ride, an
eight-hour day at the typewriter, and an evening with a TV dinner.
These women too may find their satisfaction in moments of friendship,
small comforts, and in a sense of doing their work well. For both
pre-industrial and modern women, the greatest fulfillment is often the
love of a man, and the raising of their children. Expanding horizons may
bring greater opportunity for use of abilities and for personal growth, but
they bring new frustrations and pains as well. The women of ancient
Israel, with their severely limited lives, undoubtedly had their own
means of living satisfying lives.

The woman of Proverbs, in her contrast to the submissive-rebel-
lious child-women of Genesis, was more like the women that Paul met
on his journeys. Priscilla travelled and worked with her husband. She and
Aquila were named together a pair of tentmakers, friends of Paul, and
missionaries for Christ. They were Jews from Rome, a Gentile city

which undoubtedly influenced their cultural development. Their comradeship seems to have been easier and more public than Abraham's and Sarah's. Tradespeople, not aristocrats or nomadic herdsmen, this couple knew a world and experiences vastly different from those of the couple from Ur. But like them, this missionary couple was forced out of the complacent life of the comfortable home, instructed to undertake God's journey, and willingly became citizens of his greater Kingdom.

Another couple in the early church, Ananias and Sapphira, were partners in trickery, trying to cheat the new community by holding back a portion of the profits of their real estate transactions. This complicity echoes the old couples of Genesis, demonstrating that deceit is one of the enduring features of human nature. But while the guileful women of Genesis were seen as naughty children or comic tricksters, the wife in Acts shares her husband's violent death as she shared his guilty act. In Christ, woman becomes fully responsible for her actions and suffers full punishment for them.

The church's submission to Christ is an interesting parallel to the wife's submission to husband. Christ speaks of his church as his Bride. She is his helpmeet, submissive to his will, as close as his own flesh. In this image of the marriage, we may see a deeper meaning for the submissiveness of the wife. In the Bride of Christ, the submission is a willing subordination of individual will. Perhaps God's statement at the Expulsion was presented as a natural rather than a normative law, a description of the way most lives *would* be lived, not a prescription for the ways lives *must* be lived. In Christ, we see that not just women, but all of us find greater happiness in the willing submission of our will to his.

Looking back over the Scripture in the new light shed by Christ's words, we see that the wife of Genesis is indeed an image for man and woman alike: He makes us to serve him; we spend our youth preparing ourselves to be suitable vessels for his use; he fills us with his Spirit; and in the fruits of that Spirit, we know our joy and our fulfillment. It is not a matter of where we work, how beautiful we are, how wealthy we become. Even Solomon learned that the rich physical attributes of the young bride he praised so lavishly in the Song of Solomon were not so important as love. The weary old cynic of Ecclesiastes proposes: *Enjoy life with the wife whom you love, all the days of your vain life. . . .*[9] The richer conclusion to the portrait in Proverbs satisfies us even more:

Charm is deceitful, and beauty is vain,
but a woman who fears the Lord is to be praised.[8]

Biblical Notes

1. Genesis 6:5
2. Genesis 16:2
3. Genesis 16:6
4. Genesis 18:6
5. Genesis 23:2
6. Genesis 24:11, 16
7. Proverbs 25:24
8. Proverbs 31:10–29
9. Ecclesiastes 9:9

CHAPTER III

Women
Without Men

If we view the ark as the housewife's grimmest nightmare, we must judge the flight from Egypt a close second. The women gathering and sorting their meager possessions and borrowing their rich neighbors' treasures, not foreseeing that their trip would last forty years, must have pondered the comparative merits of value and utility. Though we soon discover that they took all their own and their neighbors' gold, precious cloth, and jewels, we suspect that they also took their sturdiest and most useful pots, their warmest covers, and their most treasured mementoes.

In all this scurrying about, we find our focus drawn to a woman who is not noted for her domestic abilities, one who was neither wife nor mother—Miriam. The single woman is a curiosity in Scripture. More often when we meet a woman alone, we follow the experiences of the poor widow or the alienated prostitute. But Miriam (whose name may have characterized her: "fat, thick, strong, or bitter") was both single and self-sufficient. We must not let stereotypes of spinsters mislead us to the assumption, however, that her name actually portrayed her, for she may well have been slim and sweet. Generally, however, the centrality that most civilizations give to the woman who is beautiful and useful, fecund and desirable, tends to warp the image of the woman who is plain and independent, not supportive to man's desires or activities and not an adjunct to his career or his future generations. Secular literature often parodies her as a grotesque perversion of femininity; Scripture is more generous in giving her a small but significant role, indicating that human beings are worth more in God's eyes than man's, that God judges by different criteria.

Miriam is spoken of as the sister (possibly a half-sister) of Moses and Aaron, and is usually considered the oldest of the three. Taking into account the remarkable traits of her brothers, one can hardly wonder that Miriam also proved to have a strong character. Her youth was very different from the lives of the earlier nomadic wives. She was born of a slave people in the rich and cultured land of Egypt. Undoubtedly, she was accustomed to dwelling in a hut rather than in a tent, living in a crowded settlement rather than in the open countryside. The simple tunic of the Egyptians, the headband holding the long dark hair in place, the thong sandals, may well have been her style as well.

Wall drawings picture the clothing and hair dressings of these slave people and of their sophisticated masters. The segments of Hebrew and Egyptian history that overlap are much more fully documented pictorially than those recorded only by this iconoclastic people who have adhered strictly until modern times to the commandment against graven images.

Miriam surely grew up in an atmosphere of sorrow. Joseph had long since died and had been forgotten by subsequent Pharaohs. The Hebrews had followed the pattern of many immigrant groups: Having come as economically useful guests, they settled down and gradually metamorphosed into a threatening minority. The group flourished, some retaining parts of their own culture and religion in this alien land (though not enough to satisfy Miriam and her family), appearing to the Egyptians as a hostile ethnic group whose very prosperity and growth were ominous. *Behold, the people of Israel are too many and too mighty for us,* the Pharaoh told his people. *Come let us deal shrewdly with them, lest they multiply, and, if war befall us, they join with our enemies and fight against us and escape from the land.* [1] So Miriam knew from birth a land where her people were seen as potential enemies, and were *afflicted with heavy burdens.* These traditionally shrewd and proud people must have chafed at the servile labor. Having come as aristocrats, relatives of the head of state, they were reduced to slavery, including the building of store cities for the Pharaoh—not for their own people, not by their own choice, not under their own leaders. The heavy burdens, the sweat in the intense heat, the sting of the lash, the increasing enmity of the overseers must have made these slaves pitiful and disheartening caricatures of their proud heritage.

Added to these burdens was the knowledge that Israelite babies were threatened, that the women labored in vain, even in childbirth. Apparently, few Hebrews remembered the God of Abraham, Isaac, and Jacob; and few turned to the sure refuge of prayer and worship. They were a forgetful people who had gradually integrated much of their worship with that of the Egyptians. (Scholars see each of the plagues as an attack on one of the Egyptian pantheon.) The abiding protection of Jehovah was reduced by many to a superstitious acceptance of magic. When Pharaoh ordered male infants killed at birth, the midwives pretended that the children were born before they arrived because they feared the God that protected the Hebrews. But eventually the Pharaoh's determination to exterminate the race did result in the killing of a number of the baby boys, leaving girls like Miriam to mature in a population that was largely female. Intermarriage with Egyptians may have been a possibility for women in her situation, though such marriages are not noted in Scripture, and as we have seen, the Hebrews were reluctant to marry outside of their faith. Furthermore, slave-master marriages were uncommon in any culture; the master could simply take the woman without any legal preliminaries. In the polygamous society of Miriam's day, she could have followed the path of Leah and Rachel, and become part of the household of a Hebrew man, but slaves seldom have the means to afford the luxury of multiple wives. Whether by choice or by fate, Miriam remained single. Undoubtedly, a number of women in her generation and the following ones found they shared her situation, and probably a number of spinsters were among the sojourners in the wilderness, though no woman would have been alone. Her clan would have been responsible for her.

Miriam was like her ancestors in her concern for family. She was a descendant of Levi, close to her mother when Moses was born, probably privy to her mother's plans for the basket in the bullrushes, and certainly the one who was trusted to stand by and make good their plan. Though she and her mother used devious methods, like Rebekah, they used them for family and nation. A servile people learn trickery, discovering that sympathy can accomplish what logic cannot. She appealed to the sister of the Pharaoh—another apparently childless woman, perhaps also a single woman, by using an actual baby for bait, rather than an abstract and colorless plea for mercy. This is evidence of a mind wise in human psychology. The additional device of suggesting that the mother serve as wet nurse made possible the child's nurture in Hebrew custom and faith along with his education as an Egyptian. Miriam did more than save her brother's physical life; she helped prepare him for his role as leader, thus actually performing the usual role of mother.

Miriam is early seen to be clever, resourceful, loving, and faithful. But nowhere does it say she is pretty or gracious. And the bright woman born into a patriarchal society soon finds that beauty is more to be coveted than wisdom (all of Solomon's protestations to the contrary). Woman's traditionally domestic activities contrast dramatically with man's freer, more adventuresome ones. Simone de Beauvoir, in *The Second Sex,* traces this pattern from conception through life, noting that woman's role is frequently confined or restricted "to a narrow round of uncreative and repetitive duties . . . in contrast to the freedom to engage in projects of ever widening scope that marks the untrammeled existence."* Man thus has the role of creating values, thereby molding society and shaping the future. Curiously, it is woman, in a male-dominated society, who shares with God the anguish and frustration of working through others—in her case, usually through a husband, a lover, or a son—rather than working directly. The spinster, unable to act directly, and unfurnished with husband or son to serve as instruments of her will, must look in other directions. Miriam responded to her restrictions by dedicating her talents, her strength, and her commitment, to her brothers.

Traditionally, the single woman has found her role one of substitute mother or teacher. Without children of her own, she spends her maternal love on children of others—often brothers and sisters, nieces and nephews. Having less of the honor and less of the affection shown her than the real mother, she is often unusually sensitive to the transience and frailty of her position. This may make her either philosophical or possessive, depending on her respect for the child's will and destiny.

Miriam must have hovered solicitously over Moses in the early years, unable to claim her relationship, but unwilling to relinquish his

*Simone de Beauvoir, The Second Sex, *translator's footnote, p. 58.*

care to others. She, along with her mother, must have had some hand in teaching him of God, preparing him to be a spokesman for Israel in the palace of the Pharaoh. When her teachings and his sensitivity bore unexpected fruit in the murder of the Egyptian, she must have been heartsick—proud of his defense of the Hebrew, frightened and distressed at the consequent threat to his own life, saddened by his long exile in Midian.

In those years of preparation, his marriage, and his awakening to his destiny, Miriam had no apparent share. She must have had misgivings about his marriage to Zipporah, who was not a Hebrew woman. It was probably hard for Miriam, now middle-aged and without the comforting presence of parents, to see her beloved Moses bring another woman into his life. This wife, Zipporah, and her father, Jethro, appear to have been devoted to Moses, providing wise counsel and support for his faith, yet Moses' wife, compared with the outspoken Miriam, receives scanty scriptural notice. The focus on sister rather than on wife in Scripture is unusual, suggesting the really remarkable abilities and actions of this woman.

With thrilling anticipation, Miriam must have watched Moses and Aaron unite their talents and insights to plead the Hebrew cause before the Pharaoh. Their masculine prophetic stance contrasted powerfully with her earlier, servile feminine device to save the tiny man-child, Moses. Miriam was probably now (if the parents were dead) the woman of the house, comforting the brothers as they returned discouraged after each failure, sharing their excitement in this adventure with God. Aaron had wife and children, as did Moses, but they both seem to have relied heavily on their sister, who shared some of their prophetic powers. In that last month, which was to become the "beginning of months," Miriam must have watched the slaughter of the unblemished lamb, perhaps chafing somewhat because the younger brother rather than the older sister was considered the head of the household, and because even God himself demanded that the unblemished sacrificial animal must be male. Nothing female could suffice or atone. Considering her love of Hebrew tradition, such ideas probably seemed natural and right to her.

That final week in Egypt, they killed the lambs and sprinkled blood on the doorposts, roasted the flesh, and ate it hastily with unleavened bread and bitter herbs. Eventually, every bit of food and every God-given direction were to assume enormous symbolic importance for these people. The Passover was to become an annual celebration full of food symbolism. This symbol-making was hardly unusual for the Hebrew housewife. Every herb, vessel, animal, or action had its deeper meaning for her—to be codified gradually by dietary laws and by Scripture. The mode of killing the animals and of preparing, cooking, and serving each food was enormously important, thus enriching the significance of otherwise menial chores. Everything that went into a Hebrew's mouth was full of meaning that outweighed its value as food.

This Hebrew focus on food and drink has interesting parallels in the New Testament. Jesus too saw the symbolic meaning of bread and wine, spoke of problems of putting new wine in old skins, argued about spending his miraculous abilities on making wine for a friend's wedding. The food symbolism is less exclusively related to females in the Jewish tradition than in most other, for the Law carefully stipulated the selection of and preparation of foods. Both men and women knew how to cook, though very probably the men cooked only when women were absent. The relative importance of food symbolism to the Hebraic tradition (downgraded by Jesus' admonition to Martha about the better choice) suggests that in the earlier days this was honorable and holy work, demonstrating concern for God's Law, gratitude for his gifts, and pleasure in sharing those gifts with others. Many women still find that the growing, choosing, cooking, storing, and serving of food has great meaning for them. The industry and imagination that they spend on cakes and sauces demonstrate both skill and love. The pleasure in watching others enjoy the food and growing strong from it is adequate compensation for the work. Society has often judged a woman's worth by whether she can bake a cherry pie rather than whether she can write an epic poem. As other skills become more commonly accepted criteria for measuring social worth, the women whose vocation lies in the kitchen may increasingly feel old-fashioned and ignored. As fast-foods become the norm and leisurely family meals are replaced by snacks grabbed on the run, women are losing interest and ability in the culinary arts. The shared meal has long been the daily communal rite that allows the family to enjoy one another's experiences and ideas. The loving preparation provides the cook an outlet for creative experimentation. The Hebrews' sensitivity to the value and ritual of eating, though exaggerated, was based on a rich understanding of human needs. Whether men or women prepare the meal, serve it, and wash the dishes, the shared experience has value for the individual and the family.

Very often the Hebrew woman participated in worship by preparing the instruments and the elements while the men performed the service, thus making food preparation an act of worship. Miriam must have come to see her role in this talented family as a human parallel to the Divine: she prepared (with God's blessing) her brothers Moses and Aaron as instruments of worship. Independent of her control, God chose them to confront, lead, teach, and minister. Years later, she and Aaron were to unite in anger against Moses, insisting on being noticed, but in these early years, Miriam was apparently content to see her brothers lead her people while she assumed the dutiful role of supportive sister. At this crucial moment in the history of God's people, she was able to prepare the way (as a kind of female John-the-Baptist), and then step back and let Moses and Aaron lead.

The evidence is clear that Miriam's happiest time was during the triumph of her people and her brothers. In their joy, the liberated Hebrews sang out, and having witnessed the miracles of the Lord, Miriam took her timbrel and led all the women in a dance and a song.

> *And Miriam sang to them:*
> *"Sing to the LORD, for he has triumphed gloriously;*
> *the horse and his rider he has thrown into the sea."*[2]

This song of Miriam's is the first recorded poetic outburst of a Hebrew woman. The words are hardly feminine: They echo the longer "song of Moses," which precedes them and have the tone of war poetry. Nor is it clear that they are of Miriam's composition, though they do provide some justification for calling Miriam the first Hebrew poetess. The song bursts from a heart full of joy at the magnificence of God and the salvation of her people. She echoes her civilization when she delights in the pain inflicted on her enemies, a delight the Psalms also echo. The totality of the jubilant expression is impressive—words and music, instrument, and dance—not the solitary artist, but the leader of women in a spontaneous community celebration.

If Miriam's role in time of triumph was to lead the women, perhaps she also had a role when the water and the food grew scarce. The grumbling among this "stiff-necked" people must have at first disturbed the visionary Miriam. The people quickly blamed Moses and Aaron for taking them away from homes that grew increasingly beatific in memory, but Miriam, whose faith was a product of years of preparation rather than a moment of enthusiasm, must have loyally defended her brothers and shared their pain and disappointment with the people whom she had worked so long to save. The quail and the manna elicited no recorded songs from Miriam or from the other Hebrews, who grew increasingly accustomed to miracles and hardened to God's blessings.

The return of Zipporah, Moses' wife, along with his sons and his father-in-law Jethro, must have increased Miriam's isolation, making her feel superfluous. As Jethro became Moses' confidante and counselor, Miriam was consulted less and less. The busy Moses, concerned for his people's governance, reconciled with his family, and finally overwhelmed by his mountaintop experience, would have had less time for his sister.

The nurturing role has the inevitable anguish of being outlived, unless by some perverse process we should strive to and succeed in keeping the object of it a perennial infant. The normal child learns his lessons, the adolescent breaks from the teacher of the home, and the adult chooses new associates to provide advice in new areas. While the older Moses might return to his sister-tutor for old times' sake, he would rarely ask a woman's advice on ruling his people. She could teach him about his culture and his faith, but Jethro would be a more proper advisor for the mature man. Miriam would eventually share neither Moses' tent nor his secrets.

One of the sad effects of woman's role in the home is the limitations it imposes. Usually it is the woman who lavishes attention on the very young and the very old—the helpless extremities of humanity. Washing, dressing, feeding, cleaning, comforting are time-consuming and exhausting chores. They have their emotional and psychological rewards. But they do little to cultivate deeper and more abstract powers of thought and judgment. The devoted mother thus frequently discovers that the growing child loses interest in her conversation and respect for her judgment. Many mothers try to develop with their children, and many today seek their own second vocation after their youngsters leave the nest. Knowing that the loss of the fledglings is inevitable, the wise woman lets them go with grace and turns to discovering the new miracles life holds for her. Unless she grows, she finds that she is obsolete at forty, frustrated at her exclusion from the concerns of her family, irritated by the condescension in their voices, and confused by the change.

In Miriam's case, the historical circumstances were against her fuller development. Hebrew history and culture excluded her from a central position of leadership or worship, separating her from her brothers. Miriam, along with the other women, was to hear of the Commandments and the plans for the tabernacle in a public meeting. She would have seen without surprise that the elders were all men, and that the chief priest was to be still another man, her brother Aaron. But Miriam of the prophetic powers and poetic ability, is not mentioned. She would have been expected to join with the other women in the sewing of those prescribed lavish priestly garments that the men would wear. The splendor of the robe, the coat, the turban; the rich gold, blue, purple, and scarlet stuff along with the precious stones might have brought her some aesthetic pleasure. Joining with the other women in baking the shewbread that they could neither minister nor eat must have reminded her of those earlier days in Egypt when she prepared the way for her brothers' ministries. Or perhaps, Miriam felt a vague discontent that was nameless because her age had not taught her that women had rights before God and (unlike modern women who seek to become priests) she never had had any real expectations for service in her own right.

No mention appears of Miriam's role at the celebration of the Golden Calf—a sorry travesty on the earlier celebration of the parting of the Red Sea. Perhaps by now Miriam had grown old and tired and had seen that leadership was for the young or masculine. Her earlier leading of the women apparently did not satisfy a need for a larger role in her people's destiny. She knew her talents and she knew her dedication and believed that man or God had frustrated her real destiny. The last sad mentions of Miriam show her embittered at Moses. Soured by his leadership (or his neglect of her) and her failure to see the Promised Land, the aging Miriam with her brother, Aaron, finally spoke out publicly against Moses, saying, *Has the LORD indeed spoken only through Moses? Has he not spoken through us also?*[3] And the Lord turned angrily on the bitter Miriam and her brother, rebuking them. While Miriam had had her visions, God explained, Moses had conversations with God "mouth to mouth." No "dark speech" for Moses. The old prophetess, already shamed by her presumption and God's sharp contrasting of her dim visions with Moses' clear insights, was then stricken with leprosy "as white as snow." Aaron, her co-conspirator, pled to Moses for her, and Moses in turn prayed to God for her recovery. But God would not relent and relieve her before she had had seven days of punishment. The people, acknowledging their respect and love for the old spinster, halted their travels and waited for her recovery before they started out again. In a perverse way, her punishment indicates her stature: those to whom much is given, of them much will be demanded. Little was expected of Rebekah or Rachel, so their iniquities went unpunished. The magnificent Miriam, who could sway others to her mind, deserved even stronger punishment than Aaron. God struck her with a disease from which others by training and by instinct withdrew, underscoring her ostracism for committing a crime against God's community and his chosen leaders. At last, a woman was treated like a man and punished like an adult.

She, like the others, died before she could enter the Promised Land. *And the people of Israel, the whole congregation, came into the wilderness of Zin in the first month, and the people stayed in Kadesh; and Miriam died there, and was buried there.* [4] Her brothers' deaths were soon to follow hers in the painful litany of loss, leaving the Hebrews stripped of three giants of the faith. We assume that, by then, she was reconciled with her brothers and with her own destined role, content to be among those whose work prepared the way for the Hebrews who would inherit God's promise.

Beside Moses, Miriam was dwarfed, but placed next to the mass of humanity, this prophetess, poet, counselor, and sister had enormous stature. Her faults were the faults of a strong and talented woman. Her virtues were triumphs over adversity. Her example shows the wisdom, insight, and strength of character that can grow from rocky and apparently barren soil.

In Miriam we see the problem of subordination spelled out clearly. In an orderly world and an orderly universe, there is a system of subordination and coordination. At that moment in human history, having revolted against the system of subordination imposed in Egypt, the Hebrews, free to establish their own order, were in desperate need of leadership. God ordained that, for the time being, the woman's role must necessarily be subordinate—as was the priest's and the people's. No people can march through the wilderness to the Promised Land with confusion in the ranks. They needed a clearly designated leader, one who spoke unequivocally for God. The lesser leaders took orders from him in a chain of command. When the leader of the women or the designated leader of worship decided to be the chief-in-command, she was like a hand trying to be the head. Like Sarah, Miriam seems to have been running ahead of God's will, insisting on the gratification of her ego rather than on Israel's welfare. This was not her weakness alone; Paul later was to say that these people were denied entrance into the Promised Land because they would not rest in the Lord. A competent and intelligent woman, who has managed her brothers for so many years, would find self-reliance a barrier to such acceptance of God's will and his help.

Not all moments in history are perfect for democracy. Milton sardonically notes that Hell (or Pandemonium, its chief city) is a democracy, while Heaven is a theocracy. No one votes on God or decides whether he or she would prefer to be a cherub or a seraph. One critic notes that God uses relationships on earth as training to prepare us for relationships in heaven. If so, then subordination is a lesson all mankind (male and female) must ultimately learn.

Nor does subordination necessarily imply inferiority. The equation of these two concepts has precipitated much of the outrage in the women's movement. Although God noted that woman would be subordinate to man, he never said that she was inferior. And if the pain of childbirth and the sweat of labor can gradually be overcome, the all-encompassing law of subordination may also be diminished in time. Dante provides a beautiful response to the problem of subordination in the *Paradiso*. When the poet reaches one of the outer realms of Heaven, he is disturbed to meet a maiden who was brutally forced to violate her vows. Angered for her, he insists that she is being mistreated in her lowly placement. But Pia is delighted to be in Heaven, insisting that all Heaven's citizens are in the presence of God and require no greater blessedness. This parallels Jesus' response to the mother of James and John, who sought positions of authority for her sons in the Kingdom. Jesus answered, saying that his Father must make the decision because God's choice admits of no challenge. We must accept his will to use us as he chooses and accept authority as a trust which we use to his greater glory, not an honor that reflects on us.

We know that Miriam had a great impact on Moses. When Zelophehad's daughters made their remarkable plea for equal rights in the absence of male heirs, Moses did not hesitate to grant them. He apparently did not need to be convinced that women without men could manage estates and lives; Miriam had taught him.

Interestingly, the Greek form for the Hebrew *Miriam* is *Mary,* and it is to another Mary that we now turn our attention. Both Mary of Bethany and her sister Martha appear to have been single women; and even after all the centuries that intervened between them and Miriam, they seem to have shared many of her choices and frustrations.

Obviously the crowded cities and towns of the Roman-dominated Palestine were very different from the Egyptian slave clusters or the encampments of tents in the wilderness. The houses were more comfortable, the food and clothing more varied, and money a more common substitute for labor or barter. Yet even in this more specialized, civilized, cosmopolitan world, women continued their unchanging ritual of drawing water, baking bread, and washing the feet of their guests. No less than today, the woman's preparations for a guest indicated the hospitality of the home. In Martha's and Mary's cases, as in Miriam's, the sister substituted when the wife was not available. Since Lazarus lived with his sisters, we assume, that they, like Miriam, were spinsters who kept house for their bachelor brother. Or Martha may have been a widow; her home, her wealth may have been left to her. The sisters do not really seem to have been dominated by their brother Lazarus or dependent on him.

A few of the New Testament women appear to have worked outside the home (Lydia, for example), but the pattern was apparently still not common among middle-class women. Nor would many jobs have been available to them. Jews still seemed to have held unmarried women in low esteem. However, with the settled urban life, one senses a little more freedom for the women. Certainly women are quoted more often in the New Testament than in the old. They appear to work at some crafts either alone or with husbands. Women who were widowed were still used as examples of poverty (the widow's mite), but they seem to be somewhat freer to move from place to place without being bound to the home or being considered harlots. The wife of Proverbs did go out and manage her textile and vineyard businesses, but the women of Jesus' day seem to have gone farther afield. A group of women followed Jesus from Galilee to Jerusalem, apparently forming a regular supplement to his disciples. Perhaps they were under his protection, but with limited funds, they must have had to rely often on the hospitality of strangers.

Like Old Testament men, Jesus met women at wells and in the homes of friends, but he seems to have known more women than most of the prophets and to have viewed their problems with more understanding and compassion. He healed one woman who had been hemorrhaging for years, another possessed by demons, and cleansed the life of the woman at the well. The naturalness of his speech with women—changing in no manner from his speech to his disciples—and their enthusiastic response to him suggests that they found in him a remarkable sensitivity to their humanity. He spoke to the Samaritan woman, to the prostitutes, to a widow, a wife, to young women and old ones freely and affectionately.

His interactions with Mary and Martha are excellent examples of Jesus' relationship with women. It would seem that both sisters knew and loved Jesus and enjoyed having him as a frequent guest in their home. They do not appear to have waited for their brother to invite him.

Now as they went on their way, Luke tells us, Jesus *entered a village; and a woman named Martha received him into her house.* [5] This suggests that Martha (perhaps the older sister) was the originator of the family's close ties with Christ and the closest friend of Jesus; or it may suggest that she was in charge of the housekeeping operation and therefore was the one empowered to issue invitations, for both the invitation and the house are labelled "hers." Jesus, who apparently loved visiting friends and enjoyed talking with a small congenial group over food and drink in the evening, accepted the invitation. When he came into the home, he found that Martha *had a sister called Mary, who sat at the Lord's feet and listened to his teaching.* The younger sister responded to the welcome visitor with an open delight at his words, while Martha, the good hostess, scurried about in the preparation of the food. This labor of love apparently seemed unrewarding when compared with Mary's experience of enjoying the company and the conversation.

Contrasting Old Testament stories of wives eavesdropping on masculine conversation, this New Testament scene indicates that women were coming out from behind the veil into a more open social scene, though hardly a liberated one by our standards. The picture is remarkably cosy and warm to be a part of the usually austere holy Scripture: a young girl sitting on a straw mat on the floor near the feet of a young male visitor, who talked of travel and friends and ideas, and who opened for her a world of experience and thought. Her pleasure in the moment apparently blinded Mary to the growing fury building in Martha, *who was distracted with much serving.* Or perhaps Mary chose to ignore the warning signs of mutterings and clattering of dishes and angry door slams. Martha finally turned to Jesus, interrupting this happy exchange with her understandable but self-serving and quarrelsome complaint. *Lord, do you not care that my sister has left me to serve alone? Tell her then to help me.* Martha obviously believed that woman's role was to serve men, not to listen to them and enjoy them. She saw work as a virtue required of the good woman. And assuming that Jesus would agree with this traditional view, she sought his authority to order the derelict sister, who might have ignored her complaint, to return to her womanly duty.

Jesus quickly summed up the situation by differentiating the roles the two women had selected: Martha, the doer of good deeds; Mary, the seeker of the living Word. Ironically, the virtues of the traditional good woman, lauded in Proverbs, were now seen as potential vices. In her early rising and strenuous effort, she might miss the prize of life and its joy. Christ, who turned men's codes topsy-turvy, upset the good woman as he had done the Pharisees. Her absolute adherence to the rules of life had become Martha's vice. Having a well-cooked meal on time is surely less important than listening to the precious words of her friend and Savior. At another time, Jesus rewarded those who ignored their hunger for dinner by performing the miracle of the feeding of the five thousand. The meal gathered and eaten in the field, shared with neighbors, or properly cooked and properly served is nothing more than a physical renewal of the body so that the spirit can go on feeding on the true Word. A meal shared with family or friends is an opportunity to talk and to enjoy one another or, in Jesus' terms, to turn water into wine. But it should never interfere with the real values of the human life, which transcend what we eat and what we drink and wherewithal we shall be clothed.

In medieval times, the two women were seen as symbols of the active life and the contemplative life, the two paths to salvation. Moderns insist that they are inseparable for true blessedness, that good action follows necessarily from true faith. But Mary's way, the faith, must come first. Jesus answered Martha by chiding her in a loving but firm manner. *Martha, Martha,* said this good friend in the gentle tone of one who combines impatience with affection, *you are anxious and troubled about many things; one thing is needful. Mary has chosen the good portion, which shall not be taken away from her.*

After centuries of expecting women to bake the bread while men talked business, the Jews at last produced a man who thought a woman was foolish for stirring the stew when she could have been discovering the faith. At another time, in another place, Jesus told another woman that he could satisfy her thirst with living water. For all of his pleasure in sharing hospitality, he never thought the food itself so important as the fellowship. The Last Supper is the classic example of this; for here the bread or cereal sacrifice is symbolic of the body, the wine of the blood sacrifice. For despite the profound symbolism of the bread and wine, the real meaning came in the Communion itself—the closeness of the disciples to Christ that night, from which Judas the traitor to love must be excluded. Sharing their Last Supper together was an act of love and a symbol of the coming supreme act of love on the cross, tying it to the sacrifice of the paschal lamb. Later Paul was to fuss at the Corinthians for forgetting the meaning of the communion meal and turning the love feast into an occasion for gluttony and lust. Whatever God gives to man, even for worship, man can pervert and destroy.

Women had for so long spent so much of their energy on "many things," as had men in a somewhat different manner, that they needed Christ's lesson: "One thing is needful." And that "one thing" was and still is a redeeming faith in Jesus Christ and a living relationship with him. Men and women alike were admonished that life is more than raiment or food or other transient treasures of the flesh.

Thus did women find in Christ a liberation from their long slavery to the tyranny of the flesh. So much of their lives had for so long been given over to simple survival in those dawn years of mankind's existence, to the feeding, clothing and caring for others in the early days of civilization; and so little time had been given to cultivating that divine spark which we saw burst forth in Miriam. It was indeed a miracle that Mary still sought the light. Miriam and Mary attest that single women, though deprived of many of the natural joys of life, may have abundant compensation in other spheres.

When woman's life is defined by household chores, she is incredibly restricted in her humanity. She is judged by her economy, her cleanliness, and her efficiency. Some aesthetic pleasure may come from making an attractive cushion, or preparing a gourmet meal; and for a married woman or a single one with a real calling to such work, the household life can be very satisfying. But for many single women or for those married women who have other talents they prize more, such a life, defined for them by society, can be a prison. Martha apparently found some pleasure in her work and in sharing her home with visitors, but Mary apparently had other needs. Meals are seldom a delight when prepared for oneself and eaten alone; work is seldom rewarding when it is assigned rather than chosen. Christ, and later on Paul, realized that women possess a wide range of talents and differ among one another as much as men. These men succeeded in bringing women to their faith in part because they recognized their individual differences. They were able to look at each woman anew, without the myopic vision of stereotypic expectations or cultural preconceptions, but with a genuine concern for that woman's individualized image of God.

The lesson of the better way was apparently not lost on Martha, whose strengthened faith, in time, led her to believe Christ was capable of raising her brother from the dead. Jesus, we are told, loved "Martha and her sister and Lazarus" and knew the minute that Lazarus had died. He immediately returned to comfort and aid his old friends, arriving at Bethany after Lazarus had been in the tomb for four days. This time Martha appears to have been the impetuous one, rushing out to meet him while Mary sat in the house. Her great love and faith again made her tone seem quarrelsome: *Lord, if you had been here, my brother would not have died.* But her faith was yet full of hope as she told him, *And even now I know that whatever you ask from God, God will give you.* [6] Her words hint at a hope that he might still help because of his special relationship with God. Martha had apparently taken time after all to listen to Jesus and to learn from him. These are the clear insights of a woman with a good mind, capable of profiting enormously from the Lord's conversation. What a tragedy if she had been excluded from those wonderful moments with Jesus. As he catechized her, she recited for him his own teachings regarding the resurrection, leading him to carry the thought a step farther by adding, *I am the resurrection and the life; he who believes in me, though he die, yet shall he live, and whoever lives and believes in me shall never die.* Having heard no response to this impressive claim, Jesus turned to his friend, as if to be sure she was in agreement with him, and asked, *Do you believe this?*

Her answer was a moving declaration of faith, parallel to Peter's. *Yes, Lord; I believe that you are the Christ, the Son of God, he who is coming into the world.*

This time Martha put things in their proper order: the faith first, then the activity. It is only after this beautiful private conversation between the two good friends that they walked on into the village and to the house where the sobbing Mary sat among her sympathetic friends. She rose quickly and ran to Jesus, fell at his feet in her more theatrical manner and ironically repeated the reproachful words of her sister, *Lord, if you had been here, my brother would not have died.* The echo of Martha's statement suggests that the sisters had talked this over between themselves and blamed Jesus for his failure to respond to their plea during those bleak days of mourning. The sisters had sent word to Jesus earlier of Lazarus' illness and apparently were hurt and angry at him for ignoring their summons. Friends who comforted them added to their pain by that typical sadism of the comforter, saying: *Could not he who opened the eyes of the blind man have kept this man from dying?* This could have been an innocent question or a helpful remark, but it smacks of the sly cruelty of friends, one of the perennial disappointments we have all known in human nature. These people may have considered Jesus bad company for the good sisters and therefore have used the comment to drive a wedge between them. Or they may have been jealous of the women's friendship with the famous prophet-preacher, who talked with them as if they were men and of importance. They may have had any number of motives—protective, loving, mean, or envious —all unconsciously mixed together.

Jesus responded to the sorrow, the suffering, and the hurt of his friends. He used this moment to glorify God. These skeptical Jews were to become witnesses to the greatest miracle of Christ's ministry, and the sisters were to be recipients of Christ's great blessing.

They all went to the tomb, and Jesus wept—perhaps for Lazarus, perhaps for the sisters, perhaps for sin and death resulting from Adam's fall, and perhaps for the foreknowledge of his own tormented time to come on the cross. *Then Jesus, deeply moved again, came to the tomb; it was a cave, and a stone lay upon it.* The scene is like a dress rehearsal for Easter. Firmly, Jesus ordered, *Take away the stone.*

At this great moment in human history, Martha hesitated, considering not the power and the glory, but the smell. A woman who spent every day in the constant war against spoilage, buying only what she could use that day, cooking the meat before the heat destroyed it, eating it shortly after preparation, thought first of the putrefied flesh and opposed Jesus: *Lord, by this time there will be an odor, for he has been dead four days.*

Jesus' response was to her faith, not to her practical concerns: *Did*

I not tell you that if you would believe you would see the glory of God?
And she allowed him to do things his way at last—the perennial lesson
that Sarah and her kindred, the bossy women and men of the world,
must invariably learn. One finally must "rest in the Lord," letting God
have his way no matter how it violates our common sense.

The miracle of the raising of Lazarus followed, a miracle which
echoed the curing of Miriam. But this time, unlike the case of Miriam
and Moses, the brother is restored through the efficacious prayers of the
sisters. In fact, the sisters so dominate the scenes with Christ that we
know Lazarus only by name and as the object of the miracle, not for any
of his words or deeds. In Christ, the world was turned upside down.

The friendship continued to flourish, and Jesus returned to visit
with them. Again, at another supper, Martha served but without the
busyness and complaint, and Lazarus joined the party. After all, Jesus
had not insisted that Martha desert her kitchen, only that she not make
it her altar. Mary, ever the extravagant and dramatic member of the
household, in a gesture of love and gratitude, took a pound of *costly
ointment of pure nard and anointed the feet of Jesus and wiped his feet
with her hair; and the house was filled with the fragrance of the ointment.*[7] Mary in her unembarrassed love of Christ, found a solution to
the curse of Eve. Not concerned with her subservience to the male, this
beautiful woman abased herself enthusiastically, not as a slave but as a
worshipper giving her whole being to the Master. The costly ointment
was the lavish gesture of an impetuous woman. And the miserly quarrel
about using it came from Judas, not from Martha.

The single girl in ancient times must have been a real outcast.
Where women were a commodity to be bought and sold, where they
were valued by their husbands or sons, but not for themselves, there was
no role for the single woman. As a young girl, she was a potential wife
and mother; as an old woman, she cherished memories of her family.
But the mature woman without husband or child was a social misfit. In
polygamy, she could be the supernumerary wife. In slavery, she could
be the bond servant. But, outside of these, there seems little role for the
woman who had no marriage offers and who rejected harlotry.

Certainly there were almost no jobs. The business woman of Proverbs was a wife, though her "maidens" were perhaps employed for
money or were bond servants. The household industries of weaving and
spinning were tied to families. So she would doubtless have stayed with

her disappointed parents as the resident drudge, or with her brothers as their semi-slave. Laban's eagerness to get Leah married was undoubtedly echoed in a number of houses. In other civilizations, women could tutor the children, but in Hebrew culture, learning was a male-dominated activity. The limitations for woman in early Hebrew culture are underscored by the harsh life that Ruth knew when she was widowed. Merely to survive, women required the guardianship of men. Thus, Hebrew law demanded that the kinsmen protect the widows; in some cases they were expected to marry them. And lonely women often became prostitutes, pariahs that only Christ could love. Apparently Christ responded to their full humanity, not valuing women for beauty, wealth, talents in the kitchen, children, or husbands, but loving the pilgrim soul in them. He made no comment that suggests any desire to possess them, but calls them friends and treats them as friends.

In Mary and Martha, we see women of less talent than Miriam— not poets, not leaders, not prophets—but women fulfilled and thrilled by their experience of friendship and faith in Christ. Their portraits are fuller, the drama more extended, detailed, humanized. We have fewer gaps to fill in with our imaginations. This is not surprising, considering the much more abbreviated narrative patterns in most of the Pentateuch. The slower pace and richer detail of the Gospels allow fuller portraits of a wider range of people. Mary and Martha are remembered, not as family or heroines, but as friends Jesus loved, visited, and taught. They demonstrate in their brief scenes in his story the impact Christ had on people who knew and loved him. For they discovered a meaning in life that transcends the limits of woman's circumscribed existence and endows the bread and wine with significance. And in them, we see that the last may be the first in the richer equality of God's Promised Land, which they were enabled to enter.

Biblical Notes

1. Exodus 1:9–10
2. Exodus 15:21
3. Numbers 12:2
4. Numbers 20:1
5. Luke 10:38–42
6. John 11:17–44
7. John 12:3

CHAPTER IV

Woman as Temptress

It is disturbing to notice how often we characterize women not by personality or talents, but by their relationships with men. The old maids of the previous chapter, the wives, the maidens, and the widows are all labelled by whether they are pre-, mid-, post-, or sans marriage. In a marriage-centered culture, the shortage of men due to male infanticide or war or other situations encourages polygamy at one stage of civilization, and fraternal responsibilities to widows at another.

The widow in the Bible is usually characterized as poverty-stricken, the object of pity whose greatest happiness must lie in remarriage. Ruth's reward for her work, love, beauty, piety, and fidelity is her marriage to Boaz and the consequent new beginning.[1] Occasional widows, such as the one who served as hostess to Elijah, seem especially strong or blessed. Lydia, the seller of purple in Acts 16, is believed to have been a widow who found a way to support her household by her profitable industry in a female-oriented business. In fact, some believe, as noted earlier, that Martha was a widow, thereby explaining her wealth.

Generally, in Scripture and in the life of any culture, one of the greatest sources of happiness a woman can know is the long and love-filled marriage to a good man. But the most colorful stories grow out of distortions of this simple formula: living with a man one does not marry, marrying a man one does not love, loving a man to whom one is not married, or loving and marrying a man who turns out to be a villain. Thus, we find the further categories of women: the prostitute, the temptress, and the adultress. They are all male- (and sexually-) oriented concepts, based on the abuse of woman's relationship with man. Surely, each of these women pictured in this reductionist manner must have had other facets to her personality, other drives, other talents.

Woman, like man, no sooner had her sexuality than she started abusing it. The typical interpretation of the temptation in much of popular medieval literature was that the original sin was lust (though a few insisted that it was gluttony). Many believed that Eve used her physical attractiveness to convince Adam to sin, and a few even interpreted the Fall itself as the discovery of sex.

Though this notion of "knowledge" seems unnecessarily limited, and this notion of the Fall painfully simplistic, Scripture does indeed focus on sexual history. Genesis has numerous examples of sinful sexual knowledge, usually with woman as temptress and man as victim. There are Lot's two daughters, who, fearful of the future of mankind, tricked the drunken old man into sleeping with them. And there is the wily widow Tamar, who posed as a prostitute (i.e., she "covered her face") so as to lure her father-in-law into performing his familial obligations.

Woman is, of course, occasionally victim as well. But, women who were raped, such as Dinah or Tamar (Absalom's sister) are seen less as wronged individuals than as symbols of the violation of family honor. The law was ambiguous in the protection of woman from rape: She must have been a virgin, and the event must have occurred in the country where her cries could not have been heard. Then the man, if not already married, was expected to marry her (hardly a reward for her or a punishment for him, in her view, though perhaps in his) and to pay her family the bride price (50 shekels of silver). If he could not marry her, he still owed them the money. (If she were betrothed, the rapist was put to death.) The rape victim herself was graciously excused from penalty unless she were found guilty of harlotry, in which case she was put to death.

Given such fragile protections, only the single woman particularly determined to pursue a career in prostitution would chance much flirtation before marriage. Among the ancient Jews, the women seem to have had little opportunity for mingling with men outside of the family before marriage, and arranged marriages seldom involved much courtship. They were more business arrangements, parallel to corporation mergers. Cases of incest (as Lot's daughters or Absalom's twin sister) did occur, and brother-sister marriages may have been allowed in certain cases, so the rules of rape/seduction might still apply.*

There is a classic comment that prostitution, which was undoubtedly part of the life in Sodom and Gomorrah, was an accepted cultural pattern of both the Hebrew and the pagan world. In fact, the worship of pagan fertility goddesses (Asherah, Astarte, and Aphrodite, as this diety of female sensuality was variously named) required a period of temple prostitution for the maidens. Prior to marriage, they would wait in the temple prepared to sell themselves to the first worshipper who approached.† Certain cult prostitutes not content to discontinue this activity after their initiation into sexuality, continued the ritual throughout much of their lives. Some critics suspect that poor Hosea was married to such a woman. Certainly it would explain his equation of harlotry and paganism, though the comparison works on other levels as well.

The Hebrews fought hard against the Caananite and other foreign fertility cults that cropped up in their midst, but both Baal (the male god) and Asherah (the female) were tenacious adversaries of the stern and jealous Jehovah. And of the two, it was Asherah who more often survived even the cleansing ministrations of great reformation movements. Baal's priests at one point were destroyed, while Asherah's continued their rituals in their sacred groves.

Such information is barely hinted in much of Scripture, which is the record of God's people and their victories over such pagan seduction. Scholars of comparative religion have sifted out the references and quite convincingly cite evidence of Asherah's great power among the Hebrews. Scripture is more likely to abbreviate its notations on other religions to their abuses, their defeats, and their errors. Given the single-

---

*Sex and Love in the Bible *by William Graham Cole contains a summary with Scripture references to document all of the variations of law and practice dealing with harlotry, rape, fornication, and adultery.*

†*Raphael Patai, in* The Hebrew Goddess, *documents this fully, using hundreds of references from* Old Testament and rabbinical writings.

minded focus of the Scripture and its purpose, this selection is quite appropriate. The careful delineation of other views might lead the readers into the tantalizing worship of these pagan deities rather than the sterner adoration of the one true God. Tolerance of comparative religions seems not to be a quality one is likely to find in either Old or New Testament Scripture.

Later on, in Christian times, it was Diana or Artemis whose temple was the corrupting influence among the worldly Corinthians. One of Paul's hardest battles was to convince these people that Christian love and Christian use of sex are different from and superior to the pagan. The Ephesians, accustomed to worship of their many-breasted fertility goddess, saw Paul's message as a threat to their religion and their livelihood (making cult statues). They rushed by the thousands to their great theatre and shouted out their praise: "Great is Diana of the Ephesians!" Only Mary, who came to that same city years later, could tame them and change them by showing them another meaning of love. The goddess of the flesh is invariably at odds with the God of the spirit and the flesh, and her disciples cannot be his.

That great sensualist Solomon (whose later life was perverted by the influence of his pagan wives, leading him deeper and deeper into the allurements of Asherah) at one time knew that the beginning of wisdom is the fear of the Lord* (assuming, of course, that he was the author of that part of Proverbs). Speaking as a man who had been there, he warned against the "loose woman" whose lips "drip honey." He warned his son that *her speech is smoother than oil; but in the end she is bitter as wormwood, sharp as a two-edged sword. Her feet go down to death....* [2] Vividly, he described the meeting of the naive young man and the *adventuress with her smooth words. Passing along the street near her corner, taking the road to her house in the twilight, in the evening, at the time of night and darkness.* [3] In this twilight hour, the violent hour of lust, or hidden by darkness, the errant youth seeks out the temple prostitute, succumbing to her allurements:

Critics differ as to the extent of Solomon's authorship in Song of Solomon, Proverbs, and Ecclesiastes, but here I have chosen to use the traditional view of his authorship and set aside the debate, since the authorship has little significance when considering the value of the words, and since God uses Solomon or Lemuel or anyone else with equal ease.

And lo, a woman meets him,
  Dressed as a harlot, wily of heart.
She is loud and wayward,
  her feet do not stay at home;
now in the street, now in the market,
  and at every corner she lies in wait.
She seizes him and kisses him,
  and with impudent face she says to him:
"I had to offer sacrifices,
  and today I have paid my vows;
so now I have come out to meet you,
  to seek you eagerly, and I have found you.
I have decked my couch with coverings,
  colored spreads of Egyptian linen;
I have perfumed my bed with myrrh,
  aloes, and cinnamon.
Come, let us take our fill of love till morning;
  let us delight ourselves with love.
For my husband is not at home;
  he has gone on a long journey;
he took a bag of money with him;
  at full moon he will come home."

(Notice that she has a wealthy husband and a luxurious home, but enjoys the lust for its own sake.) Then, in his experience and wisdom, which apparently could not save him from a parallel fate, Solomon portrayed the mesmerized youth following the sly seductress as *an ox goes to the slaughter,* not knowing that it will indeed cost him his eternal life. With enormous perception of the full meaning of such seduction, he insisted, "Her house is the way to Sheol, going down to the chambers of death."

This wisdom was also the tragic discovery of Samson, who found himself the victim of such a woman. In fact, Samson appears to have been the archetypal male victim, repeatedly seeking his own destruction at the hands of loose, foreign women. In spite of his wise parents' objections, the young Nazirite insisted on marrying a daughter of the Philistines. Because the foreign woman was invariably a threat to the religion of the Jew, wise parents encouraged their children to marry among their own people. But the headstrong Samson would have his way.

The nameless wife proved a ready tool for her cunning kinsmen, who counted on her fear and her weakness. Instead of a simple negotiation for the bride-price, or the usual open handed generosity at the wedding, Samson undertook a riddle and a trick, to which his new kinsmen responded with their own trick. *On the fourth day they said to Samson's wife, "Entice your husband to tell us what the riddle is, lest we burn you and your father's house with fire. Have you invited us here to impoverish us?"*[4] The woman, pressed by these furious relatives, with whose brutality she was apparently already acquainted, feared for her life and for her family. Rather than confiding in her new husband, she accepted the terms of the threat. She apparently expected no help and sought none from either Samson or her family; and in this lonely and fatal moment, the young bride resorted to girlish wheedling. Any fool could have discerned Samson's enormous attraction to her, an attraction so powerful that after seeing her once, he had opposed his family to marry her. Counting on this and not considering the probable effect on her marriage, she used a series of feminine tricks: She *wept before him,* then she accused him of not loving her (*You only hate me, you do not love me*), and finally she fixed the desired information as the key to the proof of love (*You have put a riddle to my countrymen, and you have not told me what it is.*)

His weak response, that he has not even told his parents, did not begin to satisfy the wheedling wife. For seven days, the days of their marriage feast, she continued weeping and begging. No man could handle that, and certainly not one so lusty as Samson. . . . *and on the seventh day he told her, because she pressed him hard.*

Her response was immediate. She told the secret to her countrymen, who used the riddle against him. His consequent anger, resulting in the slaughter of thirty men, led the wife's parents (with some reason) to believe that the marriage was over. With no reference to consulting either Samson or his wife, she *was given to his companion, who had been his best man.* This passive voice verb suggests not only her impotence in any arrangements for her own disposition, but also a casualness about marriage and divorce. The parents, assuming that this outraged groom was unlikely to return to the scene of the betrayal, considered their daughter divorced. His long absence, probably a time for recovery and healing, ended with his return to his in-laws with a gift in hand, and a perfunctory announcement, *I will go in to my wife in the chamber.* The girl's startled and frightened father tried to explain his actions and placate the outraged Samson by offering him a younger, fairer sister, but Samson was not one to accept substitutes. He declared war on the Philistines, burning their crops with flaming foxes and slaughtering a thousand people with the jawbone of an ass.

Certainly such an experience should have been enough to cure the youthful Samson of any temptations toward foreign or sexual entanglements, but strong Samson, ever weak in the flesh, went first to a harlot in Gaza and finally to Delilah. Meanwhile, the wife's story ends in catastrophe: Bought by Samson, used by her kinsmen, disposed of by her parents, she was nothing more than a pawn in the hands of others. Her single moment of free choice resulted in her decision to manipulate her new husband, a decision which surprised no one in that day or this. He was apparently ready to forgive her, perhaps not even expecting loyalty or integrity from a woman. One suspects men thought of women with the condescension and affection one feels toward any domestic animal, complicated of course by lust. Certainly the property that was woman could not have been expected to think or act on a human level. Even today we are often shocked at the punishment of a female criminal, as if women and children should not be held accountable. But the gradual growth of women's acceptance as full human beings has forced us to accept their full accountability and responsibility.

The death of Samson's wife at the hands of angry Philistines infuriated Samson. His property was lost to him, and those responsible would pay the price. Nothing is said of her punishment or his sorrow, suggesting that both Samson and the Philistines saw her simply as property, not as a thinking, separate, responsible individual. It is hard to discern the image of God in the lineaments of such an unthinking victim.

Delilah is not designated as wife, but simply as *a woman in the valley of Sorek, whom Samson loved.*[5] She was a smarter and probably older woman, motivated somewhat differently in her perfidy. This time, the betrayal was of "love" (at least on his part), not of marriage; and it was explained by money, not fear. The wording is parallel, but Delilah seems to have been more cynical and the lords of the Philistines were not her kinsmen, therefore had no emotional hold on her. Their request, which catered to her materialism, they justified by military and patriotic motives: *Entice him, and see wherein his great strength lies, and by what means we may overpower him, that we may bind him to subdue him;*

and we will each give you eleven hundred pieces of silver.

Delilah, the cynical manipulator of sensuality, was thus more of an actress in the drama than was Samson's wife. Her choices were deliberate and calculated, and Samson's resistance this time seemed more playful than real. It is hard to understand how any man could have been tricked by the same woman four times, especially after his earlier experience with his wife. Samson can only be characterized as a slow learner. Delilah's shrewdness was also obvious here: She approached the question quite directly—no tears this time. She tested out the information he fed her, but apparently with sufficient discretion that he did not notice the *men lying in wait in an inner chamber.* She used his feelings for her to shame him in his treatment of her: *Behold, you have mocked me. . . .* This is evidence of a proud woman whom Samson enjoyed teasing, but whom he was eventually required to satisfy. Her final device was the classic emotional blackmail available to the "weaker" partners: *How can you say, "I love you," when your heart is not with me?* She then escalated the nagging (*pressed him hard*) until, as in the scene with the earlier woman, *his soul was vexed to death.* At last he revealed the secret of his Nazirite vows and his uncut hair.

The shrewd woman, recognizing this story by its ring of truth, called her co-conspirators to pay her for fulfilling her part of the bargain. Her eye was apparently on the money all along. As a cynical business woman, she probably suspected their reluctance to pay up after she had fulfilled her portion of the bargain. Then she agreed to help with the haircutting herself, an indication of a tough, unsympathetic, even vindictive heart.

Her evil shines out most clearly in this scene which combines gestures of love and of betrayal in a blood-chilling foreshadowing of Judas' kiss: *She made him sleep upon her knees; and she called a man, and had him shave off the seven locks of his head.* To catch a man at his most vulnerable moment in the trusting pose of relaxation against her knees, in the impotent state of sleep, and then to destroy his strength by stealth and cunning is crueler than outright attack. Using the weapons available to the physically weak woman—her beauty, her masked cleverness, her coldness, her knowledge of his love, and his trust and weakness—she won her perverse victory.

Milton saw this as the siren face of woman. Enticing man with her apparent love and modest acquiescence, she turns into his beautiful entrapper. He attributes this quality to women generally, pondering the reason God had for creating such a gorgeous monster as the young witch:

> . . . *such outward ornament*
> *Was lavish't on thir Sex, that inward gifts*
> *Were left for haste unfinish't, judgment scant,*
> *Capacity not rais'd to apprehend*
> *Or value what is best*
> *In choice, but oftest to affect the wrong?*
> *Or was too much self-love mixt,*
> *Of constancy no root infixt,*
> *That either they love nothing, or not long?*
> *What e'er it be, to wisest men and best*
> *Seeming at first all heavenly under virgin veil,*
> *Soft, modest, meek, demure,*
> *Once join'd, the contrary she proves, a thorn*
> *Intestin, far within defensive arms*
> *A cleaving mischief, in his way to vertue*
> *Adverse and turbulent, or by her charms*
> *Draws him awry enslav'd*
> *With dotage, and his sense deprav'd*
> *To folly and shameful deeds which ruin ends.*
> 　　　　　　　(Samson Agonistes, *IV, 11. 1020ff)*

Thus, not Delilah alone, but all women, Milton believed, found their triumph in the subtle entrapment of man, the inevitable adversary. Confused by his lust, her beauty, and his presumption of her innocence and ignorance, man is easily ensnared by the wily and lovely female— for contrary to Keats' assertions, beauty (physical beauty at least) is not truth.

So Delilah had her classic victory: *Then she began to torment him, and his strength left him. And she said, "The Philistines are upon you, Samson!"* She was there to watch her shorn lover, like Gulliver among the Lilliputians, attempt to "shake himself free," to discover the weakness of his muscles; she saw him seized by Philistines, who gouged out his eyes. Here, the reader wonders about the depth of Delilah's viciousness, the degree of relish or disgust she felt when this bloody ritual took place. Certainly, to many people over the ages, her combination of beauty and evil, her allurement to destruction, which parallels the sirens and witches that Odysseus knew on his journeys, are symbols of the vicious side of female nature. The archetype of the young witch, who allures only to destroy the hero, whether she be the Lady of the Rocks (Lorelei) or the Lady of Situations, as Eliot calls her, is the frightening contrast to the idealized lady of romance, who leads man to a discovery of his highest self. This wicked woman, like Circe, the queen of the Lotus Eaters, lures man to his ease, distracts him from his calling, and vulgarizes or castrates him. The multiple forms that the Delilah figure has taken suggest that it is one of the concepts of the female which haunts man and frightens him. She is no harmless plaything or mindless drudge; she is a real threat to his masculinity and his mission.

The point-of-view of the narrative continues to be primarily masculine, ignoring Delilah's responses and focusing on the other Philistines and on Samson. If she, like the other Philistines, saw this as a national and religious victory (*Our god has given Samson our enemy into our hand*), Delilah may have considered herself a patriot and a worshipful servant of her gods. We know her only from the masculine and Hebrew viewpoint, and therefore can surmise little about her motives and her personality. She is not mentioned in Samson's death scene, when the newly revived Samson pulled down the temple on himself and on his enemies, but surely she knew of it or even witnessed it. Her hold over Samson is broken with her perfidy and his blindness to physical beauty. Blinded prophets are traditionally those with the deepest spiritual insights.

Ironic justice would have been served by having her in the midst of the enemies exterminated by the penitent Samson, but like other women, she had no explicit punishment. So clever a woman must have finally experienced some kind of a recognition; a time must have surely come when she looked at her blood money, as did Judas, and discovered a sour taste in her mouth. But in Delilah as pictured, we perceive no feminine softness, no sympathy or remorse. She was as hard as any man, as shrewd and as conniving.

In this willpower and in this perversity we see the lineal descendent of Eve. In her deadly mixture of beauty and venom, this clever enchantress was more sinister than the easily identified masculine forms of malice. Not that men invariably eschew subterfuge, but Scripture and life show it to be the more effective weapon of woman. As Eve invited Adam to taste and so to fall, so Delilah invited Samson. But unlike Eve,

Delilah had no recorded motive to justify her evil, and no remorse.

This is undoubtedly because she was a foreign woman, and foreign women in Scripture are usually presented as incapable of human decency. They tend to have been unmitigated and unmotivated in their evil. Like Jezebel, those who worshipped their alien gods were enemies of Jehovah and therefore were viewed as demonic. Certainly the cruel and lascivious practices of many pagan religions made this understandable. The foreign men, when they worshipped foreign gods (like Nebuchadnezzar's lieutenants) were equally evil. Scripture is not so tolerant of paganism, heresy, or apostasy as are we. Perhaps the especial distress at a woman's evil was a result of the condescending and simplistic expectation of her virtue and her compliance. After all, Eve fell when Adam did. We should expect no more virtue from her than from him. When a woman uses all her allurements, her training in the sensual arts, and her natural power over men in the service of Ashtoreth, she is more effective against the male than a battlefield full of armed men. They can kill a man's body, but she can pervert his faith and his will.

Hosea's harlot-wife Gomer is a most spectacular scriptural example of the perverse foreign woman. In spite of her loving husband and her three children, she turned (or returned) to the lure of prostitution. If she was a cult prostitute of Astarte, performing the ritual coupling to honor the marriage with Baal and to increase the land's fertility, she certainly provided a threat to Hosea's faith as well as to his marriage. The cult prostitute (as noted earlier) would have lain with strangers for hire as Gomer did. Hosea also spoke of the feast days of the Baals, when Gomer burned incense to these wooden gods of fertility and decked herself with jewelry and went after her lovers. Hosea rightly saw this as apostasy as well as adultery. She forgot her husband and her God, believing that the Baals and the lovers provided for her sustenance when, in fact, God provided everything.

Hosea's loving act of forgiveness and his welcome to his wayward wife is an impressive reversal of the usual unrelenting hostility to any such evil: *And the LORD said to me, "Go again, love a woman who is beloved of a paramour and is an adulteress. . . ." So I bought her for fifteen shekels of silver and a homer and a lethech of barley. And I said to her, "You must dwell as mine for many days; you shall not play the harlot, or belong to another man; so will I also be to you."*[6] Thus did Hosea, the loving husband, forgive and redeem the wayward wife, making of her a symbol of whoring Israel and of himself a symbol of the loving and forgiving God. As in the submission relationship, we see here the husband-wife love as a dim shadow of the greater love of God for humanity. The love tie broken here (hésed) by the adultery was deeper than the legal bond of marriage. It was the loyal love that binds two parties in a covenant relationship, a loyalty arising out of the relationship itself.*

Certainly Hosea, even if he seemed arrogant and self-righteous when he portrayed himself as an image of God, nonetheless had greater love of his wife than did Samson. He was less worried about her threat to his faith than her moral and intellectual confusion and her redemption. She did not trick him; she simply betrayed their love, a deeper hurt by far. Thus, Hosea's loving welcome home contrasts dramatically with Samson's perfunctory return to repossess his property. His subsequent devastation of the countryside, endangered and finally destroyed his young bride. In contrast, Hosea, in his selfless act, presaged the redeeming love of Christ.

The manner of the narration of these stories is quite different, demanding different reading. Samson's story has all the formal marks of a folk narrative built around a popular hero. His prowess in battle is colorfully contrasted with his clumsiness in love. The events of his life are whittled down to encounters in war and in love, with little of his wisdom or faith apparent in the selection of events. The description of the marriage, in its sinful and carnal emphasis underscores the dangers of marriage outside one's religion and nation. The description of Delilah's perfidy reinforces this lesson while pointing to the heartlessness of foreign women. The focus, selection, and ordering of the events of the narrative indicate that this is a moral fable, built on the instructive experience of a flawed national hero. The lesson in female psychology (or in what they considered alien female psychology) is as picturesque as the admonitions of the Proverbs. Such lust will tempt man and bring him to physical—and potentially to spiritual—ruin.

The Hosea narrative is far more individual, the experience of one man who seeks to understand his life symbolically. The words appear more those of one author, the vision is more unified around the image of the beloved harlot wife. The parallel between man and God is drawn

*Bernhard W. Anderson, Understanding the Old Testament, p. 248.

more clearly, the narrative is less important than the message. The central character is important for his understanding rather than for his physical prowess. There is less story here than philosophy; the book exhorts and explains rather than narrating or characterizing. The first-person experience becomes more intimate and intense than the third-person, observed event. We watch Delilah in action as a part of exciting history, developing our own judgments with a little help from the narrative pattern and tone. Hosea's wife is perceived from the throbbing lover's words, portrayed as the source of his anguish, known only through his impassioned responses. Hosea involves his reader more deeply because his great love and his denial of his own pride are closer to the problems and challenges we know ourselves.

Woman often seemed devious in Scripture, while man remained decent. Both man and woman were presented as self-seeking, inclined toward evil, insensitive to other humans and to their Maker. But society and nature have provided woman with claws within the velvet glove that invariably surprise and outrage man. In recent days, we have encouraged more forthrightness in woman by making the pattern of plain-speaking and openness more socially acceptable, though hardly popular universally. Now a woman may be allowed to admit she is ambitious or angry while earlier civilizations expected her to smile through her frustrations and pain. Her admissions in no way make her more admirable, but they do allow her more open use of her weapons and talents. Even today, most people are not comfortable with the idea of woman as antagonist or sensualist. The prevailing image is one of frailty and innocence, and any violation of this ideal is still disturbing. The admission that a woman enjoys sensual pleasures and indulges them still shocks many people.

The foreign woman was not the only problem for the Hebrews, threatening their terrestrial peace and their eternal reward. Man might find temptation on the next rooftop, nonchalantly bathing, apparently oblivious of its own power. The woman might have been the wife of one's friend, a Hebrew and a neighbor. David found his temptation to be thus.

As usual, the scene is presented from the man's point-of-view with minimal insight into or interest in the woman's motives, emotions, understanding, or development. The story this time is more in the manner of history. David was important as the greatest king of Israel; his role as lover was important in the development of his personality and his faith and in the procreation of his line. The Bathsheba narrative showed only one side of his nature, but did not dominate his life as Delilah's did Samson's. Sadly, the woman herself is often known only from the single act, as Bathsheba is known from her compliant adultery, and not as a fully developed human being. But history is not interested in individuals unless they leave their imprint on a society, as David did Israel. Hebrew Scripture also selected those historical events that demonstrated the power and the love of God. In this narrative, the focus is on David, a warrior, a poet, a man of God, the leader of Israel, into whose hands God had entrusted his people.

The story is presented as an atypical interlude in this great warrior's career, a time when he was unwell and discontented with life. In the springtime, *the time when kings go forth to battle,*[7] David had sent his men off while he remained at Jerusalem. Considering David's fame in battle, this unaccustomed lethargy marks a weariness with his life and his wars. The quiet of the warrior-free city, the isolation from his battle friends, and the balmy weather seem to have bred in David a curious torpor, as if he awaited a new experience. And then Scripture tells us: *It happened, late one afternoon, when David arose from his couch and was walking upon the roof of the king's house, that he saw from the roof a woman bathing; and the woman was very beautiful.* Springtime, boredom, and finally (again in the twilight hour), lust.

The affair demonstrates that in all things David was a man of action: He inquired about the woman's family and her husband, imperiously sent for her, and without preliminaries (or at least none on record), "took her." Perhaps it was a seduction, probably the affair itself was extended, but little is indicated of her response. A beautiful woman, bathing where she might have been seen by the king, may well have baited a trap for him, though Scripture says "it happened," as if by chance rather than intention. David's imperious demand along with his impressive person must have flattered Bathsheba. Certainly she made no move to notify her husband as a woman of honor would have done. Scripture does say, "she came to him," not indicating any force on his part, and then "he lay with her." The ceremonial cleansing mentioned (*Now she was purifying herself from her uncleanness*) may well refer to a bathing after childbirth or her menstrual period. (*If a woman conceives, and bears a male child, then she shall be unclean seven days; as at the time of her menstruation, she shall be unclean.*—Lev. 12:2) But by the time Bathsheba conceived by David, she was clearly his conspirator. She turned to him with her message (*I am with child*) apparently expecting him to help her handle her problem.

The following events, in which David sought to trick Bathsheba's husband Uriah into sleeping with Bathsheba and thus cover his shame, must have confused and hurt the woman. No woman could consider it romantic of her lover to push her betrayed husband back into her bed; and if she were in love with David, Uriah must have become repellent to her because of her combined love and guilt. But adding to this insult was the husband's surprisingly unchivalric nobility—refusing to sleep with Bathsheba while his country was at war and his men sleeping in tents. One suspects that Uriah's stern moral stand struck Bathsheba as troublesome and tiresome. His cool control must have contrasted dramatically in her mind with David's hot lustiness.

The plot to kill Uriah seems to have been David's, though Bathsheba must have been suspicious and relieved. She circumspectly and perfunctorily—or perhaps even genuinely—*made lamentation for her husband.*[8] However, when genuine feeling is involved, Scripture more often uses the more picturesque word "wept." The formal phrase, "made lamentation" implies the ritual lament for the dead, involving wailing and weeping and beating one's chest. The shallowness of her feeling is ironically suggested in the following sentence, *And when the mourning was over, David sent and brought her to his house, and she became his wife, and bore him a son.* Bathsheba must finally have wept with relief as she had not wept with grief: rid of her wronged and threatening husband, saved from public humiliation and even the threat of death, married at last to the king, and safely delivered of his son.

A memory of their crime must have cast an occasional shadow on their bliss, like a small cloud on a sunny day, sending a cold chill through them both. A Hebrew woman with the whole tradition of her faith behind her could not share Delilah's clear conscience. Had nothing else disturbed her world, there was always the stern Nathan. This old thorn in David's flesh appealed to his sense of destiny, his basic decency, his love of God, and his tender conscience. Finally, the penitent David was driven to public confession, which must have been a public humiliation for Bathsheba. His eloquent psalm of remorse must have been from her point of view an embarrassing advertisement of their illicit affair.

But even more painful than this public recantation by her eloquent and extreme husband must have been the pathetic death of their child. The anguish of the sickness, the joining with David in prayers over the tiny boy, and watching together over his doomed little body must have shown Bathsheba still more of her husband's multi-faceted nature. The lusty lover and the remorseful penitent was also the gentle and loving father, the comforting husband. Surely the loss of the infant must have drawn them together in their common love for this innocent victim of their guilty adventures.

After the child's death, David cleansed himself, accepted the justice of the punishment, and turned to comfort the mourning Bathsheba. Their marriage now surely became more than simple animal magnetism. Their love, which later bore Solomon as fruit, was blessed by a forgiving God, and continued into their old age. Bathsheba was able to win David over to her will even in his dying moments, thus procuring the throne for their second son.

In her old age, the widowed Bathsheba apparently expected to have the same power over the new king, her son Solomon, but her charms had diminished by then. The loving son was outraged that his mother sought to come between him and his favorite bed partner. This ironic final mention of the aging beauty, with her son following the path of lust mapped out by his parents, points to Jeremiah's poignant summary of such a life: *The fathers have eaten sour grapes, and the children's teeth are set on edge.* [9] No action so involved with the will, so negligent of others, can stand alone. The human race draws heavily on the experiences and choices of its ancestors. Thus, the whole history of Israel is tainted by the *abominations, . . . adulteries and neighings . . . lewd harlotries* [10] of the royal house. Bathsheba's seduction was a sign of the corruption in the life blood of Israel. And she lived to see Nathan's dire prophecies come true.

In each of these cases, foreign women or Hebrew, harlots or adulteresses, the women were seen primarily as instruments of men's corruption, but seldom as their unwilling victims. Susanna of the Apocrypha did appear as righteous in her struggle for virtue, starkly contrasting with Bathsheba's easy compliance, but she was a rare instance. Usually, the unnamed fallen woman appeared, performed her ritual temptation, corrupted her victim, and was forgotten or stoned.

It is in the New Testament that we finally see an altered attitude toward such women. Jesus, the friend of publicans and sinners, stood beside the adulteress asking that "he who is without sin" cast the first stone. He quietly revealed to the woman at the well that he knew of her "husbands," discussed faith and worship with her, and set her on the path to redemption. Though we do not know that Mary Magdalene was a harlot, tradition has pictured her as a reformed prostitute. Christ cast out her "devils" and made of her a friend and a new woman. In his redeeming love, he won her over to a life of loyal service. When all of the men but John had fled, Mary lingered near the foot of the cross. And Easter morning, Mary Magdalene was one of the first at the tomb.

Other men have made "honest women" of harlots by loving them and marrying them and treating them as human beings. Hosea loved his harlot wife, forgiving her over and over. But only Christ transformed character, making the harlot the disciple, giving her back her self-respect and providing her with meaning for her life. Perhaps this is, in part, because he spoke of harlotry forthrightly but gently, despising the sin, but not the sinner. In part, it was his enriched perception of the Law: not simply the hatred of adultery, but the analysis of the root causes of the action. To look at a woman with lust (as David did Bathsheba) is to set the machinery in motion. Christ put the burden on the initiator of the lust (most often the man, though not always) and forgave the victim most easily. His was no condescending forgiveness based on the low estimation of woman's mind, will, and conscience. Rather, he attacked the brutal treatment afforded harlots, pointing out that their partners in lust often went free. He forgave the remorseful sinner with firm directions: *Go, and sin no more.* Such stern advice coupled with keen insight into a woman's role in lust, her frequent victimization, her fear of society's response, her inability to return to decency again after her fall—these must have made Jesus a savior to the despised, and a rabble-rouser to the pious. No wonder women followed him so readily and responded so gratefully to his message of redemption.

The Old Testament tradition had been to present woman as adjunct to man's sin, seldom the main actor in the drama of Israel's history. She was the temptress who sang her siren songs, luring the godly adventurer from his path. Her own needs, temptations, adventures, and paths were subordinated to his. Delilah's last days are lost to human memory as are Bathsheba's. Only the sinister black widow Jezebel could take a commanding role in history, and only she needed the punishment commensurate with her stature.

Christ saw women more fully, not simply as causes for man's sin or as helpmeets for his work, but as humans with their own paths to salvation. He knew them to be capable of good and evil, of sin and of redemption. His solemn but gentle words to the woman at the well show that he saw beyond the sin to its source and saw beyond the surface of the fallen woman to the longing soul within. The law had failed to meet woman's need, as it had failed man's. Like the outcast woman Jesus cleansed of her bleeding, women found in his touch the gentle, compassionate, understanding godliness they sought. Bathsheba's ritual bath of purification led to an orgy of lust and death; Christ's cleansing baptismal waters redeem the sinner. Though her sins be scarlet, he can make them white as snow.

Biblical Notes

1. Ruth 1—4
2. Proverbs 5:3–5
3. Proverbs 7
4. Judges 14:15–15:15
5. Judges 16:4–30
6. Hosea 3:1–3
7. 2 Samuel 11:1–5
8. 2 Samuel 11:26–27
9. Jeremiah 31:29
10. Jeremiah 13:27

CHAPTER V

Woman as Sovereign

Though woman in Eden was granted, along with man, dominion over nature, history has seldom seen female sovereignty. As already noted, the curse of submission more often was the role for woman. Even when she was a queen, like Bathsheba, she ruled only at the sufferance of man, be he husband or son. Seldom did the power reside in her alone.

Even the famous Queen Esther was no sovereign in her own right. Neither her blood line nor her virtue, nor even her wisdom mattered so much as her physical appearance and the favor of an absolute monarch. Queen Vashti, the dethroned predecessor to Esther, seems in fact to have been a woman of strong character and considerable virtue, if not proportionate common sense. Her refusal to display herself before the king's drinking cronies, who had been on a monumental eating and drinking orgy, was an act of some courage. The monarch and his wise men agreed that her refusal to act the role of the submissive wife might cause women *to look with contempt upon their husbands.*[1] Thus the spirited Vashti was replaced by one *better than she*[2] as a lesson to obstreperous wives, and King Ahasuerus, also known as Xerxes, issued a decree that every man would henceforth be ruler in his own household —a decree easier to make than to administer.

The subsequent beauty contest was an occasion for gathering the

region's loveliest virgins into the king's harem, where they were supervised by his eunuch. Such a selection process and Esther's summons to
participate hardly suggests her free will or the king's preference for
virtue, though he did stipulate that the girls be virgins, not second-hand
property. Every step of the process points to woman as possession. The
honor of being in Ahasuerus' harem was considered adequate payment
for a life of submission.

Nor was Esther the first Jewess so enslaved. Moses would have
found no need to be so explicit about selling daughters into slavery had
the practice not previously occurred. The Jews, who wept at Babylonian
captivity had long since grown accustomed to being used as slaves by
these foreigners. Thus there is no hint of anger or rebellion in the
recorded words or actions of the orphaned Esther as she was *taken into
the king's palace and put into custody of Hegai who had charge of the
women.* In fact, she *pleased him and won his favor; and he quickly
provided her with her ointments and her portion of food, and with seven
chosen maids from the king's palace, and advanced her and her maids
to the best place in the harem.* [3] The clever girl, while winning favored
treatment from the eunuch, also kept in touch with Mordecai, her foster
father.

The whole oriental flavor of the harem emerges in the description
of ritual: twelve months of beautification (six with oil of myrrh and six
with spices and ointments) supposedly preceded the first overnight visit
with the king. And unless the king was pleased with the maiden and
requested her again by name, she would not have been honored by a
second trip to the king's bedchamber. Esther, who apparently won
everyone's affections, delighted the king, inspiring him to proclaim her
his queen and celebrate the new choice with a carnival of feasts, gift-
giving, and tax remissions.

Curiously, the beautiful Esther had seen fit to keep her nationality
and her religion secret until she won the king's "favor and grace," a
shrewd move attributed to Mordecai's advice. Also, through Mordecai's
sharp ears, she became privy to a plot against the king's life. Her protection of Xerxes at this point increased his affection for and his admiration
of his beautiful queen.

Esther consistently used her beauty along with judicial restraint and
womanly virtues to achieve her ends. At the climactic time for the Jews,
when Xerxes was prepared to undertake massive persecutions, Mordecai

fed her the information and gave her the advice she needed, stiffening her spine by noting that this was her hour for greatness and that she shared with her kinsmen the perils of the purge. Esther, realistically agreeing that she could not remain silent and safe, made the strong choice that Mordecai urges: *Then I will go to the king, though it is against the law; and if I perish, I perish.*[4] This firmness is remarkable from a young harem girl carefully trained in the arts of sensuality and submission. Like other Hebrew women whose histories we know, she snatched her opportunity for service and shone in adversity.

But Esther was no Vashti, eager to confront the king with her moral superiority. She let her beauty and her charm work for her. Whether God (who is never mentioned in this chronicle) or some other cause reminded the king of Mordecai's earlier service, Ahasuerus was already softened toward the loyal Jew before Esther arrived. Ahasuerus' pleasure in Esther's beauty and hospitality finally convinced him. Esther knew that a man is most susceptible to prodding when in the presence of a beautiful woman, after good food and drink. She also knew that he must believe himself to be the aggressor in their relationship. Though she placed herself where he would see her, she waited for his summons and later for his signal that he was ready for her petition. Esther, in short, knew the tactics of female guerilla warfare. Not the hard-pressing of Samson's women (which was effective briefly with a lustful but not shrewd man, whom they expect to leave), but the subtle pressure of the harem girl who had to rely on the munificence of a strong man for her own survival and pleasure.

There was nothing gentle or feminine about her victory. She required an 83-foot high gallows, that Haman and his sons might be hanged, and rejoiced in the slaughter of 73,510 Gentiles. The victory was Esther's, to be shared with Mordecai, her mentor, and the Jews, her people. There is no reference to God, faith, prayers or forgiveness in this book. Their fasting and their feasting seem to be national patterns, not theologically motivated. If this is a woman's mode of using power, one sees little difference between power-hungry men and blood-thirsty women. Only the modes of winning the victory vary; one displays his brute force openly, the other manipulates her advantage subtly. But both are selfish and vengeful in their human relationships.

Esther became a heroine to the Jews, not for her wise sayings, her virtuous life, or her intellectual depth, but for one moment of self-

protective heroism and a lifetime of shrewd conniving. Her victory was
the victory of a powerless underling against impressive odds, therefore
a victory that won their sympathy for the methodology and their admiration for her loyalty to the Jews. They saw her, like Deborah, as a warrior
for Israel.

Her story is a romantic historical reminder of the basis for celebrat-
ing the Purim, a festival at which the Jews were said to drink so heavily
that "Blessed be Mordecai" became blurred with "Cursed be Haman."
(Notice, they considered Mordecai, not Esther, the real victor.) This
narrative was apparently based on the memory of a threat to the Jews
in the Dispersion, and was preserved because it celebrated Hebrew
shrewdness and female wiles at the expense of the pagan enemy—that
famous and wealthy sensualist Xerxes I. Esther's portrayal combines
those traits most admired in Hebrew heroes and heroines—shrewdness
and beauty—while neglecting to mention her negative features—sensuality and duplicity. She is a fairly primitive personification of pre-Chris-
tian virtues, celebrated for her service to her people as if there were no
higher ethical value. God speaks in different ways to different ages. His
message to the Jews by way of Esther seems crude compared with his
subtle and sensitive message to us by means of Christ. But a people in
bondage seek a hero and thirst for vengeance. This young harem girl who
made a weapon of her beauty served that need.

Esther, Bathsheba, Salome, Jezebel were all royal women who
made various uses of their power: to win a throne for a son, to save a
people, to kill a saint, or to attack Jehovah himself. The reputation for
good or evil apparently lies in the goals sought, not in the methods used.
Esther did not dance in Salome's manner, but in all likelihood she
introduced all possible sensuous and sensual pleasures to convince her
king to follow her will. Her banquet was sufficiently entertaining to
entice him to return for more. She was undoubtedly a better person than
either Salome or Potiphar's wife, but somehow not quite the example
we would wish. Martin Luther is not alone in finding this book weak in
moral or theological impact.

The sinister use of power by the queen had been most vividly
exemplified in the much earlier and far bolder career of Jezebel. The
daughter of one king and the wife of another, this imperious woman
became for Elijah the epitome of evil. Like Solomon's foreign wives, she
was a worshipper of the Phoenician fertility goddess Astarte or Asherah,

whose priests and prophets she cultivated. When Elijah conducted the celebrated contest on the mountain, only the priests of Baal were massacred, not those of Astarte, who apparently continued to flourish under Jezebel's patronage. Jezebel's worship of the fleshly goddess probably accounts for her antipathy toward the stern Jehovah and his austere prophet. She and her husband Ahab apparently lived in oriental splendor, entertaining pagan priests by the hundreds (in stark contrast to God's priest, Elijah, in the wilderness being fed by ravens).

By bits and pieces we discover something of the rich lifestyle of Ahab and his queen: the ivory house, the palace harem attended by eunuchs, the feasts, and the life of sensuality (including enough wives for Ahab to produce some 70 sons). In a rare reference to make-up, we see the aging queen *painting her eyes and adorning her head*[5] before she shouted out the window at Jehu. The old harem girl could not afford to relax into aging sexlessness. If power derives not from one's father, a foreign king, but from one's appeal through the flesh, age must be compensated for with paint and careful lighting. Those who live by the flesh die daily with each new wrinkle. Gateyards and palaces, horses and chariots all point to a life far more luxurious than in the early days of the kingdom, a life parallel to the later life of the Persian monarchs traced in Esther's history.

Jezebel, recognizing that her power came not from her own right, understood that her strength lay in Ahab's weakness. In a scene vividly revealing his character, Ahab responded childishly to his disappointment when Naboth refused to sell his ancestral heritage—a vineyard—so that Ahab could use it for a vegetable garden: *And Ahab went into his house vexed and sullen because of what Naboth the Jezreelite had said to him. . . . And he lay down on his bed, and turned away his face, and would eat no food.* Jezebel showed her fiber immediately. Acting the role of maternal and dominating wife, she *came to him and said to him, "Why is your spirit so vexed that you eat no food?"* After he recounted the rebuff by Naboth, she encouraged him, *Do you now govern Israel? Arise, and eat bread, and let your heart be cheerful; I will give you the vineyard of Naboth the Jezreelite.*[6] Her voice echoes down the ages as the no-nonsense tone of the impatient but indulgent mother. She clearly had no respect for Ahab as king or as man. Not even bothering to discuss the details of the arrangement with him, she took it on herself to set a plot in motion to kill Naboth. The ease with which she purloined the king's seal and prerogatives signals her real power lying behind his splendid veneer of sovereignty.

Once again, woman, powerless without man, makes man the instrument of her will. She served no nation or clan as did Samson's women, and no God Jehovah as Miriam did, but only the idol of self and flesh. She became the archetypal witch-queen because of the unrelenting evil of her actions. Again a foreign woman, worshipping foreign gods, she displayed no hints of fleeting idealism or gentleness or love to modify her sinister mien. She was pure evil, therefore assuming symbolic value to the Jews and later to the Christians. Her image reappears in Revelation as the great harlot, and her name has become a synonym for vicious femininity.

This clever conniver arranged to use the Law of Moses for her own perverse purposes, manipulating the righteous citizens so that they stoned Naboth. When the whole action was accomplished, she notified Ahab of her victory. She ordered, in the manner of a mother producing a surprise gift for her child, *Arise, take possession of the vineyard of Naboth the Jezreelite, which he refused to give you for money; for Naboth is not alive, but dead.* Ahab asked no questions; he ran happily after his reward.

It must have been an unwelcome surprise to find the dour Elijah also in the vineyard, prepared to accuse Ahab for responding to his wife's evil incitement. The all-encompassing curse startled and frightened the king: *I have found you, because you sold yourself to do what is evil in the sight of the Lord,* proclaimed Elijah. *Behold, I will bring evil upon you; I will utterly sweep you away. . . .* Ahab heard the words and crumbled before their authority. Scripture records, *He rent his clothes, and put sackcloth upon his flesh, and fasted and lay in sackcloth, and went about dejectedly.* The Lord, seeing the sincere repentance, relented slightly *because he humbled himself,* thereby deflecting the doom from himself, but not from his progeny.

Very different was the curse and fate of the fiery Jezebel. Of her, the Lord said through Elijah: *The dogs shall eat Jezebel within the bounds of Jezreel.* The arrogant queen watched her weak husband humble himself, but disdained to follow his contrite example. She outlived him, staying on in the harem among her finery and her servants, surveying the world from her latticed window. The curse of wealth or beauty or power is the illusion it creates. The rich and beautiful queen grows increasingly convinced of her superiority and permanence as she watches others cater to her whims. It is hard to believe that beauty dims, wealth dwindles, and power evaporates. The saints have traditionally been the poor (not only in spirit), who enjoy few of the riches of this world and therefore inherit the kingdom of the next.

Jezebel was a shrewd and cynical woman, but was nonetheless deluded by her sumptuous life into believing her servants were loyal. Yet she faced her death with an impressive heroism, like an old actress sailing magnificently through her farewell performance. When Jehu came to Jezreel, Jezebel apparently recognized the signs of her impending death. She painted and adorned herself and then addressed him with fury as "murderer of his master."

Looking up at the window where she was, Jehu said: *Who is on my side? Who?* In response to his query, *two or three eunuchs looked out at him,* awaiting his command. And he said, *Throw her down.* [5]

These servants with whom she lived showed no loyalty to their mistress-queen. Seeking favoritism with whoever was in power, they responded promptly to the order: *So they threw her down; and some of her blood splattered on the wall and on the horses, and they trampled on her.* Only after the dispassionate Jehu had eaten and drunk did he consider that a king's daughter deserved a dignified burial. *"See now to this cursed woman,"* he ordered the servants, *"and bury her; for she is a king's daughter."* But when they went to bury her, they found no more *of her than the skull and the feet and the palms of her hands.* When they notified Jehu, he recalled the prophecy of Elijah: *In the territory of Jezreel the dogs shall eat the flesh of Jezebel; and the corpse of Jezebel shall be as dung upon the face of the field in the territory of Jezreel, so that no one can say, "This is Jezebel."*

The glimmer of determination we saw in Esther had flashed out in Jezebel, but to no good purpose. While Esther was faced with harem intrigues and the Byzantine political scene of Xerxes' reign, Jezebel had, in her regal hauteur, dominated her weak husband-king. In her arrogance, she saw herself as the real monarch. Though Ahab had his harem, only Jezebel is mentioned of his women. The smaller kingdom and the childish monarch provided a fertile playground for this willful woman. Undoubtedly, Jezebel's worship of Astarte (curiously, Esther's name is a variant of Ishtar, or Astarte) provided the religious basis for her activities, the philosophic basis for her perverse morality. She subscribed to the *carpe diem* philosophy that places pleasure and self at the center of life. If one covets one's neighbor's vineyard, and if one has the brains, the power, or the money to acquire it, why hesitate? Astarte encouraged the life of the flesh, a life to which Jezebel apparently committed herself fully until that very flesh was trampled by horses and her body became "as dung in the field"—a fitting conclusion for the old sensualist. As Paul told the Galatians centuries later, *God is not mocked, for whatever a man sows, that will he also reap. For he who sows to his own flesh will from the flesh reap corruption. . . .*[7]

Jezebel was a more direct manager than Esther, using less of sensual appeal, less psychology in manipulating her husband. Undoubtedly Ahab was a weaker man and king than Xerxes. The Hebrew monarch displayed none of Xerxes' despotism in his tone or actions. Thus Jezebel could play the tune to Ahab's dance, using his weakness to lead him deeper into sin. Less culpable than she, he escaped with a kinder death.

In Jezebel, we see the reversal of roles. The old prophecy of obedience seems to have been momentarily suspended. But her very strength proved a vice, leading her husband into temptation and herself into damnation. Again we find evidence that God's words in Eden were less curse than prophecy. While man would find work his fate and his nemesis, woman would find her subsidiary role the same. Man could escape work and woman could escape subordination—at a price. Jezebel's temporary primacy cost her dearly, just as Miriam's ambition had cost her. Miriam accepted her role and God's judgment, but Jezebel acknowledged no power above herself. As women increasingly find themselves in positions of power, often with men as the subordinates, they may expect some sacrifices. Certainly, as history moves toward the reversal of the old roles, we are living through the anguish of adjustment. Queen Elizabeth I found her power cost her dearly in emotional terms, but Victoria's compromise was also expensive. Men will learn in time to follow women as well as men—as Israelis and Indians have demonstrated. And women will need to be more direct, less devious. But in the long transformation, we will need to reconsider most of our institutions which have been historically based on a system of subordination. Man may learn to live with woman as equal, but he will be understandably reluctant to trade a patriarchy for a matriarchy. The discomfort involved in the new discoveries should be adequately compensated by the new world that results—if it is a world in which Miriam, not Jezebel, achieves her deserved supremacy. For all of us must finally acknowledge that power is transient and the real glory lies in God, not in man or woman. The first question facing women is how to achieve power. The subsequent questions are harder: how to use it properly and view it as a gift of God.

If one were to generalize from Jezebel and Miriam, one would necessarily see subordination as the God-given path for woman. Yet Esther led (though indirectly, and encouraged by a man) when true subordination would have made her submissive to evil. We look in vain for other women among the line of monarchs who shared the throne of Israel with their husbands, but we find only a few king's daughters who made unpleasant wives. Israel was to remain for many years a patriarchy. Perhaps other queens reigned in Israel, sharing the anonymity that history grants the decent, normal people who do their work properly avoiding dramatic virtues or vices. We know of Queen Athaliah only because she broke the pattern in a most unladylike manner, usurping and holding the throne. Most women, however, gained authority through their beauty and strength of will and wielded it through their weak and enamored men.

The New Testament furnishes us with a final example of this type of the flesh-worshipping witch-queen in Herodias. She left her legal husband, Philip, to live with Herod. When John the Baptist pointed to their open adultery and noted that their life was not lawful, the furious queen demanded his death. Timid Herod, fearing the consequences of killing a prophet and angering the Jews, would not obey the demands of his enraged bedmate. She, making standard use of the traditional devices of the female, enticed him with the lascivious dance of her daughter, Salome. Then, when the young dancer won his promise, she parroted her mother's demand. Herod, though "sorry," broke the law and his own conscience. He beheaded the saintly John and had his head brought in on a platter. In more dramatic form than her predecessors in temptation, this beautiful disciple of the flesh used man's weakness for her will. Evil can triumph where conscience is cowardly and "sorry." The stronger contrasts of the saintly man, the regal whore, and the bloody charger make this the archetypal horror story of perverse use of feminine power.

If God had left history and revelation with only these examples, we should be forced to agree that subordination is the proper role for woman. Miriam learned her lesson, Esther succeeded only by obeying a man. Herodias and Jezebel show the improper use of power usurped from men. In the midst of this parade of insubordinate and sometimes evil female misusers of authority, Scripture breaks the pattern by giving us a powerful example of a truly heroic woman. Deborah, a judge, whose story is found among those heroic tales of the judges, is a unique example of a tribal heroine. The judges appear to have gained and held authority through strength of character, not through their lineage; they were military leaders, figures with native intelligence and strength.* Thus, Deborah must have been a Hebrew version of the Amazon, an Israelite Athena to rise in such a system among such primitive people with such a strong patriarchal heritage.

In most cultures, heroism comes from putting ideals before life. Survival is not enough; humanity must prevail—over the environment, over others, over its own animal nature. The usual choice is the long, mediocre life; the heroic choice is the short, glorious one. Thus heroism usually involves physical bravery in defense of family or country or ideals. To the true hero, slavery is worse than death, submission unthinkable.

Such a code is clearly man-made. It is rooted in physical prowess and based on significant opportunities for free choice. Woman's role over the centuries seldom has given her much opportunity for such heroism. Survival was her hope, happiness her ideal. She expected submission or even slavery to be her role. A cage, after all, can be a protective fence as well as a limiting prison. Esther and Jezebel did not seek to escape from their circumscribed harem life; nor did they seem to reject the comforts of the golden cages in which they lived. Bathsheba seemed to believe herself a lucky woman, not chafing at being little more than a prized possession. Rebekah offered no argument (on record) when she was purchased. The male narrator may have failed to note their distress in the sweep of his larger narrative; after all, none of us is prepared to hear all of God's message, which is always fuller than our perception can admit. It is also possible that, in their world of limited expectations, these women felt no distress.

Simone de Beauvoir traces female perceptions of self over many generations in many cultures, concluding that woman sees her role as immanence and man's as transcendence. While man fights his battles and dies his heroic death, woman bears the children, binds the wounds,

*"Judges," Westminster Dictionary of the Bible.

and mourns the dead. Man protects the culture, but woman preserves it.*

Obviously, many women are as strong as men, some stronger than most men. Their ability to labor and endure is legendary. It is self-image and acceptance of roles that usually keeps women out of war, or at least out of uniform and out of the front lines. We expect women to minister to the needs of men, to nurse the wounded. That Deborah, or any woman, in so conservative and role-oriented a society as the Hebrew, should rise to heroic station is remarkable.

Scripture tells us a number of things about this folk heroine: she was a prophetess as well as a judge of Israel. She was the wife of Lappidoth, who apparently did not share her prophetic powers or her position, but who seems (in his very absence of notice) to have created no barriers to her activities. She would sit under the Palm of Deborah between Ramah and Bethel in the hill country of Ephraim. People came to her for judgment.

These bits of introductory information differentiate her considerably from Miriam, of whom she must remind us. Although she, like Miriam, was admired and sought out for her wisdom and prophetic powers, she was not simply an adjunct to a brother who bore the real authority. Since she apparently had a husband living at home, she surely had some home responsibilities, though no children are mentioned. This may explain why she stayed near home and let the people come to her. (We wonder if she was a working mother whose divided loyalties drew her away from home and pulled her back again.)

Such omissions of reference to spouse or children or parents are not unusual in narratives of the judges, for these are folk heroes, whose tales were remembered for their color and their heroism. Unlike the earlier patriarchs and the later kings, their mates, their children, and their parents are relatively unimportant except as actors in the heroic drama. Deborah fits easily into the formal devices that unify these stories, but she is remarkable as a portrayal of a female. In a culture where a woman is known by her role in relation to men, it is startling to find a woman whose grandeur is her own.

We soon discover also that Deborah spoke with some authority. When she summoned Barak, she spoke with a prophetic voice:

> The LORD, the God of Israel, commands you, "Go, gather your
> men at Mount Tabor, taking ten thousand from the tribe of

*Simone de Beauvoir, The Second Sex.

Naphtali and the tribe of Zebulun. And I will draw out Sisera,
the general of Jabin's army, to meet you by the river Kishon with
his chariots and his troops, and I will give him into your hand."[8]

The tone is as masculine as Miriam's war song, suggesting there is no
such thing as a feminine style. The style of the message meets the needs
of the occasion, not the sex of the speaker. The details of this message
were the practical necessities of war—not romantic or vague. The plan
was a clear strategy for gathering resources and plotting action. The
promised victory showed her conviction of the accuracy and source of
her message.

Barak, accepting her authority, believed and obeyed, but insisted
she accompany him. To this peculiar (almost feminine) stipulation, she
immediately responded, *I will surely go with you.* This remarkable
woman thus embarked on the war-like path later followed by Joan of
Arc, enlisting her soldiers, encouraging them as they marched, and
finally, leading them to battle. In the poetic rendition of the scene,
which follows the prosaic, the picture is far more vivid:

> *Then sang Deborah and Barak the son*
> *   of Abinoam on that day:*
> *"That the leaders took the lead in Israel,*
> *   that the people offered themselves willingly,*
> *   bless the LORD!"*

5:2

Deborah's quickness to respond to the call of duty paralleled Isaiah's—
"Here am I, Lord. Send me." Her zeal, in the face of her forewarning
of the dubious honor ahead, apparently put enthusiasm into other hearts
as well. From the outset, she had known that this would not be a path
to glory, *for the LORD will sell Sisera into the hand of a woman.* She
shared this knowledge with Barak, as a forthright comrade would do
before they started out together as soldiers of the Lord. Their triumphant march to the destined battleground echoes the strong parallelisms
and repetitions of Hebrew poetry:

> *LORD, when thou didst go forth from Seir,*
> *   when thou didst march from the region of Edom,*
> *the earth trembled,*
> *   and the heavens dropped,*
> *   yea, the clouds dropped water.*

This "Song of Deborah," which may not have been her composition (as Miriam's may not have been hers), is generally considered one of the oldest and loveliest selections of Hebrew poetry in Scripture. It follows the style of war poetry, describing the lawless background situation and then placing its heroine in her proper place:

> *In the days of Shamgar, son of Anath,*
>   *in the days of Jael, caravans ceased*
>   *and travelers kept to the byways.*
> *The peasantry ceased in Israel, they ceased*
>   *until you arose, Deborah,*
>   *arose as a mother in Israel.*

A woman had at last extended her sphere to encompass more than her own needs or those of her family. She had become a spokesman for God and a mother to her people. The female imagery portrays her protective role of the warrior-woman, relating her image less to Amazon queens than to the hovering Hagar. God is sometimes portrayed as the protective mother, weeping over her lost children, feeling compassion for their pain. The strong woman in this case accepts her leadership role, rides off with her comrade-in-arms, but maintains her womanly nature. The poem summarizes the gratitude of the people for her gracious offering up of self:

> *My heart goes out to the commanders of Israel*
>   *who offered themselves willingly among the people.*
> *Bless the* LORD.

Deborah's epic triumph was the triumph of the Lord and of the peasantry of Israel. She was the Old Testament version of Mother Courage. Scripture shows us over and over that beauty and power can come from unexpected sources. While we have looked in the palaces of kings for nobility, it dwelt instead in mud huts: with the young girl giving her brother to a princess, the housewife counselling her countrymen under a tree, and finally in a simple maiden bowing before the awe-inspiring annunciation of God.

The song of Deborah catalogues the troops marching to battle— the clans, their nobility, their homelands. Those absent or useless are roundly cursed as the poem chronicles the fighting. The poem firmly answers those who insist women are more peace-loving than men. If anything they prove fanatic fighters, less inclined to adhere to the formalistic man-made rules of warfare and codes of chivalry. Sisera apparently found himself no match for Deborah's and Barak's forces.

As the armies marched on with might, the cowardly Sisera galloped off to hide, leaving his army in rout. . . . *and all the army of Sisera fell by the edge of the sword; not a man was left.* Running from one woman, Sisera sought refuge in the tent of another, Jael, who coaxed him to come to her. Had she been a foreign woman, the Jews would have classified her as a temptress-witch, but in the service of Israel, she became a heroine. She *covered him with a rug,* and in the tradition of the hospitable hostess, she *opened a skin of milk and gave him a drink.* Then as he was again hiding under the covers, assured that she would protect him and lie for him, *Jael the wife of Heber took a tent peg, and took a hammer in her hand, and went softly to him and drove the peg into his temple, till it went down into the ground, as he was lying fast asleep from weariness. So he died.* In the bloodthirsty tradition of patriotic war poetry, the song triumphantly proclaims:

> *"Most blessed of women be Jael,*
> *the wife of Heber the Kenite,*
> *of tent-dwelling women most blessed."*

The woman's mode of battle continued to be sometimes devious. Janus-faced, she confounded man with her gesture of hospitality on the one hand and murder on the other. Like the innkeeper (or harlot) Rahab, she proved herself through her heroic strategy. Deborah was not described as a warrior or an Amazon, but as a leader and a strategist. Jael was the heroine of the battle, a heroine without glory because her method was too close to Delilah's. Only the country and the god had changed, not the techniques.

The concluding lines of Deborah's song bring us back to the normal female roles in warfare: as victims and mourners. Sisera's mother callously considered the fate of the enslaved maidens, and awaited the return of her son—an ironic contradiction of actual circumstances:

> *Out of the window she peered,*
> *the mother of Sisera gazed through the lattice:*
> *"Why is his chariot so long in coming?*
> *Why tarry the hoofbeats of his chariots?"*

Her wisest ladies make answer,
 nay, she gives answer to herself,
 "Are they not finding and dividing the spoil?—
  A maiden or two for every man;
 spoil of dyed stuffs for Sisera,
  spoil of dyed stuffs embroidered,
   two pieces of dyed work embroidered for my neck as spoil?"

The incremental nature of her thoughts, moving toward her own desires, her love of finery, underlines the lavish life of Israel's enemies, which like the pomp of Jezebel was to meet its destined destruction. Those who live by the sword, who loot their victims and enslave their women will find themselves victims and slaves. The war hero, as in Greek epic and Roman, is brutal by our standards. The pleasure in the gore, the cruelty in the victory, the delight in vengeance seem to us grotesque (though it is hard to compare the degrees of cruelty involved in methods of warfare). Even the Israelites, these people of the covenant promise, are thrilled with the massacre of their enemies and God's.

The poet concludes the song with a prayer of vengeance and without further reference to the principals. Sisera's mother would soon begin her lament, Jael would wash the blood out of her covers, Deborah would return to her home and her husband, and life would return to normal. In the cryptic style of Scripture, no mention is made of the obvious.

The Amazons (Diana, Joan of Arc, and Deborah) to the contrary, the role of woman has seldom been as warrior. Though she has proven herself a competent soldier, she usually fights her battles privately without military uniform. Judith enticing and decapitating Holophernes, Rahab hiding the Israelite spies—these women, like Jael, fight their battles by subterfuge. Without artillery or comrades or public display, women combine shrewd plotting with swift action to win their victories by surprise. Often lacking man's physical strength, women must use the devices they have at hand. The Hebrews apparently had then as now no difficulty in accepting the notion of women as warriors. Deborah and Jael became national heroines for their courage and their loyalty.

Whether in war, in government, or in worship, the usual Hebrew woman, however, had a small role. These women we have studied were the remarkable exceptions to the rule. Though two of these women—

Deborah and Miriam—were recognized as prophets, they were not eligible to serve as priests. Nor was Anna in the New Testament. They were, in fact, for all of their extraordinary talents, like other Hebrew women, excluded from participating in most of the worship. Even in the Jewish home, the husband and the sons led the services, read the Scriptures, and said the prayers. From Miriam on, women's roles at the tabernacle or Temple were largely supportive.

Early Christian worship apparently changed this somewhat. When Paul mentioned the diverse talents (teaching, prophesying, speaking in tongues), he referred to women as well as men. Though Jesus' disciples were all men, we have already noticed the women who drew close to him and followed him before and after his physical death. He appeared first in his resurrected form to women; and women were in the Upper Room praying with the group of the faithful at Pentecost.

One woman joined with her husband to become one of the first missionaries (Priscilla and Aquila). Another woman (Lydia) opened her home to the early Christians, brought her whole household to Christ, and (probably) labored with Paul in the spread of the gospel. Paul frequently mentioned the women serving the various congregations (the mother and grandmother of Timothy, for example) and apparently built close friendships with a number of them. The very strength of the women's voices in the early church might explain his extreme concern for their domination, which he expressed to Timothy, and his fear that this trend might lead to the overturning of the whole family structure. But Christ had signaled that loyalty to him might easily drive a wedge through the family. Subservience to husband cannot include accepting spiritual guidance from a pagan husband. And clearly women often discovered Christ before their husbands did. Lydia and others immediately turned to the task of converting their households, thus suggesting spiritual leadership. Mothers (such as Timothy's) were apparently then as now influential in the spiritual growth of their children. Such women Paul clearly respected and loved. His bleak advice on woman's role in the church must be placed in this larger context of his activities and comment. Paul, like many moderns, was struggling with the fresh vision and understanding demanded by Christ, overcoming his traditional Jewish background. And he was working among a people who accepted certain social patterns (slavery, subordination, monarchy, etc.) that we reject.

Christianity offered Jewish and Gentile women alike a new sense of importance. Christ had demolished the system of submission by his radical reassessment of values. Now the first should be last, and the meek would inherit the earth. In his kingdom male and female were to be equal, and he treated them equally. After centuries of submission with occasional glimpses of shared dominion, women found in Christ a new path. No need for either man or woman to wheedle a position on the right hand of Christ, no need to be jealous of another person's gifts.

Paul expressed this richer equality in Galatians 3:26–28:

> ". . . for in Christ Jesus you are all sons of God, through faith. For as many of you as were baptized into Christ have put on Christ. There is neither Jew nor Greek, there is neither slave nor free, there is neither male nor female; for you are all one in Christ Jesus."

Biblical Notes

1. Esther 1
2. Esther 1:19
4. Esther 3–4
5. 2 Kings 9:30–37
6. 1 Kings 21
7. Galatians 6:7–8
8. Judges 4–5

CHAPTER VI

Mary—
Woman Redeemed

The outstanding woman of the New Testament was neither warrior nor prophetess nor queen. Though she came from the lineage of David (and of Bathsheba and of Ruth), she was a simple Jewish maiden who expected to spend her life quietly in Nazareth. Espoused to a carpenter, surrounded by family, this pious virgin must have expected a very ordinary life. Her gentleness and compliance marked her from her first appearance, as does her closeness to her family, especially to her cousin Elizabeth. Gabriel had already spoken to Elizabeth and promised her a son, John. Now the angel appeared to Mary, saluting her with, *Hail, O favored one, the Lord is with you.* [1] Frightened and troubled, Mary was comforted to hear that she had indeed *found favor with God.* But her feelings must have been mixed when she discovered that she would conceive and bear a son. The angel emphasized that this child would be the Son of the Most High, that he would reign over the house of Jacob forever, that of his Kingdom there would be no end.

A woman of the lineage of David, betrothed to a man of the same lineage, educated (so far as girls were) in the history of Israel and inculcated with hopes of a Messiah, Mary was the perfect "vessel"—yet she showed her full humanity by echoing Sarah. *How shall this be?* The human response to miracles has often been argumentative. Mary insisted that she could not conceive because she had no husband. When informed that the Holy Spirit would come to her, she quarreled no further. *Behold,* she said submissively, *I am the handmaid of the Lord; let it be to me according to your word.* She, like Sarah, learned that *with God nothing will be impossible.*

Mary's first action was to visit Elizabeth, whose pregnancy was mentioned by the angel. Elizabeth recognized Mary's blessedness, and settled her heart, giving her joy in the knowledge of her conception. It may well be that the frightened girl, fearing the gossip of the community and the anger of Joseph, ran to Elizabeth for comfort and escape. She may have sought confirmation of the angelic message. But in this friend she found more than sanctuary, she found joy.

> *My soul magnifies the Lord,*
> *and my spirit rejoices in God my Savior,*
> *for he has regarded the low estate of his handmaiden.*
> *For behold, henceforth all generations will call me blessed;*
> *for he who is mighty has done great things for me,*
> *and holy is his name.*[2]

Woman, who has traditionally found transcendence in her sons, perceives in Mary the very apex of this joy. Childbirth, that blessed punishment of Eve, has frequently provided woman with her greatest fulfillment. Old Testament women prayed for delivery from a barren womb, even at the price of pain in childbirth and the threat of their own deaths. Consistently, woman saw God's blessing in her ability to conceive and bear—rightly considered a miracle. When God added to this the further blessing of a son (always more significant than a daughter in this patriarchial system), and beyond that a son who would lead his people, the women were thrilled. Thus, the mothers of Isaac and Jacob and Joseph and Moses, Samuel and Samson were all "shadows and types" of the mother of Christ. Here finally was the miracle they all presage—the miracle of the Incarnation.

At long last the image of God was to reappear on Earth unsullied by the sin of Adam. One woman, Eve, ate of the fruit of the tree and lost for all humanity the hope of eternal life. Another woman, Mary, accepted her blessedness and bore for all who would believe the promise of life eternal. Through one woman's willful act came sin. Through the other woman's humble obedience to God's will came redemption.

Somehow, because of this, we expect Mary to wear the regal trappings of the Byzantine paintings, which picture her enthroned, surrounded by adoring angelic hosts, and crowned with her beaten-gold halo. But in actuality, she probably dressed as humbly as her sister peasants, drew her water at the well, baked her bread, and wove the fabric for her baby's swaddling clothes. Like other Jewish women we have studied, she married without much notice (though some of the ceremonies could be very elaborate), and settled into her expected life without arousing comment. Scripture ignores her courtship, notes no specific dowry paid for her. This time the maiden apparently did not need to prove herself for her husband: We find no reference to her physical beauty or wealth.

This insignificant couple attracted no attention until the hand of the Lord touched them and transformed their lives. Like thousands of other Jews around the countryside, they traced their ancestry back to David and the patriarchs. But we know from the commentaries of the local rabbis that they were considered insignificant, even in a community as small as Nazareth. The focus of human activity was Rome; Jerusalem was nothing more than an outpost of this great empire; and Bethlehem was less than nothing. Caesar was the man to watch; Herod was his Hebrew minion, and Joseph of Nazareth was but a digit on the census scrolls. By any rational measurement, Joseph and his betrothed were nonentities. Their marriage could have interested only a few of their family and neighbors; their children would add only another layer of experience to the sum total of human knowledge and ignorance. Only when the world was turned upside down did man come to wonder about the young maiden Joseph married and seek to reconstruct the details of those neglected histories.

Though Joseph's piety and kindness are suggested in his sympathy for Mary and his obedience to the angel, the story, even as told in the Jewish Matthew's Gospel, is not Joseph's. This time the husband is the adjunct, the woman's story is temporarily central. But even Mary mattered only as vessel for the seed of God and nurturing agent for Jesus' early years. Her story diminishes as his flourishes. But Mary bracketed Christ's human stay. Present at conception and crucifixion, she became the archetypal immanent female force, contrasting with God-man transcendence. She attracts us as a historical figure, as a human and sympathetic image, and as a symbol of womanhood and of humanity.

Scholars tell us that Mary must have been legally bound to Joseph when they made the journey to Bethlehem. Jewish custom would have forbidden her making that trip alone with him had she not been legally betrothed. The obedient couple bowed first to the will of God and then to the will of Rome, responding to the inconvenient government edict, in spite of the impending arrival of their first child. The exhausting trip and frustrating conclusion before the innkeeper's door tested their mettle. Youth faced with adversity proves its real character. Out of poverty and pain can come love, maturity, compassion, and wisdom, on the one hand; or hardness, violence, and cruelty, on the other.

The birth of this child in the primitive surroundings of the cave-stable takes us back to the first sinful and exiled couple with their lonely experience of birth. But Mary and Joseph soon found that they were not alone. The very heavens proclaimed the glories of this child. Scripture records the picturesque visitors: angels and shepherds and wise men. Mary, we are told, *kept all these things, pondering them in her heart.* [3] The signs of childhood are inevitably the precious mementoes of the fond mother, who builds her hopes on these symbolic events. From the conception to parturition, she felt the constant presence of God. Eve had lost that closeness with God, and other women seem rarely to have heard his voice except through men. Even Sarah heard the message of the angelic visitants second hand. Yet God had consistently taken a hand in providing his people with leaders, born of women. The awareness of God's will working through woman's body is very clear among the patriarchs, the kings, some of the judges, and the prophets. But no woman could have heard God's voice more clearly than Mary. In her modesty, she seems to have spoken little and thought much. These cherished memories must have formed fascinating topics for conversations she later had with others who also came to follow her son, the Messiah.

Mary shared with Moses' mother the fear of her child's destruction by regal decree. She shared the experience of those lonely sojourners in a foreign land, as she travelled with her little family to Egypt. And she felt the peace of returning home, when she came back to Nazareth, settling there into the age-old routines of housekeeping. In her quiet life, she recapitulated the experience of countless women.

In those early years of Christ, we know only that his mother observed Jewish law and custom. She and Joseph took the child for circumcision, for training in the law, for preparation in the reading of the Scriptures. Their annual Passover trip to the Temple at Jerusalem must have been the high point of their year. Mary watched Jesus from day to day. *And the child grew and became strong, filled with wisdom; and the favor of God was upon him.*[4]

When he was twelve, a time when the Jewish boy prepares to become a man, their Passover trip took a different turn, one that brought them both worry and pride. Having discovered that Jesus was not with them on their return trip, they went back to search for the lost boy. They found him *sitting among the teachers, listening to them and asking them questions; and all who heard him were amazed at his understanding and his answers.* Mary, not Joseph, burst out in hurt protest: *Son, why have you treated us so? Behold, your father and I have been looking for you anxiously.* Forgetting her modesty in the presence of these learned men, thinking only of the worry and relief she felt, she sounded very like a mother.

In Jesus' response—a sharper answer than we might have expected, except for our knowledge of the tone that does usually develop in parent-child relations—we hear the declaration of independence eventually necessary for every young man. *How is it that you sought me? Did you not know that I must be in my Father's house?*

In these twelve years of nurturing the child, Mary had lost her sense of awe. It is hard to scrub a child's ears, bandage his cut knee, tuck him in bed, and also recall that he is the Messiah. She even called Joseph his father, forcing Jesus to remind her that he was Son of the Most High. Apparently, this confrontation was only the beginning of Mary's education. At this point, Mary and Joseph *did not understand the saying which he spoke to them.* Gently, Jesus returned to Nazareth as their obedient child, prepared to wait and to mature. Mary watched this astonishing boy, who *increased in wisdom and in stature, and in favor with God and man,* and the thoughtful Mary *kept all these things in her heart.*

Much of a woman's life is inarticulate. The recurrent phrases for Mary's silence ("kept all these things," "pondering them in her heart") suggest she was a meditative woman who mulled over the events of her life and the marks of her son's blessedness and prepared herself for his maturity. She possessed a quiet, practical thoughtfulness akin to the wisdom of Proverbs. These sayings contrasted intellectual knowledge or shrewdness in dealing with a deeper, richer wisdom which starts with the fear of the Lord, feeds on experience and observation, and flourishes on meditation. This folk wisdom, the fruit of experience, is less verbose than philosophy, less self-serving than cleverness, but more rewarding than either. Mary's life proved that she had such wisdom. This has frequently been the form of intellect developed by women, attested to by Proverbs' use of a feminine personification for wisdom. Often history has seen societies shut women off from books and schools, thereby encouraging them to develop their minds in more practical ways. The intellect can not be thwarted so easily as men would believe. Therefore, women have become the family historians, the practical neighborhood politicians, the child psychologists, the religious advisors over the years. Colleges which are now encouraging older women to return for schooling have discovered that they are often excellent students, who combine industry with practicality. Businesses are finding many women sensible, dependable, enthusiastic workers. Their wisdom, like Mary's, comes from quick minds, meditative temperaments, and years of practical experience. Considering the many centuries women were denied educational opportunities open to men, it is amazing that we have not bred the brain right out of them. On the contrary, the Greeks worshipped Athena for her wisdom. The author of Proverbs was not alone in seeing wisdom as a female.

Mary, the maturing woman, observed the maturing son as she raised her growing brood of boys and girls and worked about her home. The death of Joseph is not mentioned in Scripture. References to him cease after the visit to Jerusalem, though references to Mary continue. If he died while Jesus was an adolescent, leaving Mary a widow, his death must have saddened the family; and Mary must have thanked God for the comforting presence of her eldest son. It may be that Jesus' long delay in entering his ministry is attributable to his role as breadwinner for the household. He would have found himself responsible for his younger brothers and sisters until they reached the age of self-support. To the end of his life, he seems to have felt responsible for his mother, considering her welfare even as he hung on the cross.

The resulting closeness of the mother and son must have created a painful problem for Jesus. For no mother finds it easy to accept a son's maturity or authority, and no son is content to remain a child forever. As Mary and Jesus enjoyed the wedding feast at Cana together with his disciples, she turned expectantly to him for more wine. A tone of annoyance echoed in his voice as he responded, *O woman, what do you have to do with me? My hour has not yet come.* (John 2:4) He appeared reluctant to move ahead of God's timetable for him, to use his miraculous powers for housekeeping chores. Mary, however, expected his help and instructed the servants to obey him. He obediently performed his miracle, and his pleased mother expressed no surprise. The miracle served to manifest his glory and to convince his disciples, but it also explains why Jesus was forced to leave home to continue his ministry.

The final scene of Jesus with Mary, shrugging off the trammels of motherly concern, is in Mark 3:31–35. Mary brought Jesus' brothers with her to dissuade him. He had just faced a whole crowd accusing him of madness and demonic possession. And then his mother and brothers came, joining the crowd outside the house, and calling to him. They may, very naturally, have worried about his health and safety. No normal family cultivates heroism or self-sacrifice in its members. Most of us prefer modest success accompanied by even more modest sacrifice. The usual advice of the mother for the child is, "Be careful!" But Jesus could not be careful and be Christ. He had no choice but to deny Mary's power over his life. When the crowd sitting about him told him that his family were outside asking for him, he replied: *Who are my mother and my brothers?* Then, looking around at those who were listening to his words, he said, *Here are my mother and my brothers! Whoever does the will of God is my brother, and sister, and mother.* [5]

Christ in these words reversed the whole tradition of Judaism, one built on family ties, on tribal loyalties. If blood no longer held humans together, if the accident of birth no longer justified loyalties, then one must radically reassess his relationships. Though Jesus' responsibility for his mother and his love of her never diminished, he refused to accept husband-wife, parent-child relationships as central to life. Christ preached a God-centered life, not a family-centered one. He preached loyalty to God before loyalty to family. Finally the family became those who love God and love one another (the church). Any other system of priorities would turn him and his people away from their true mission. Jesus said, *For I have come to set a man against his father, and a daughter against her mother, and a daughter-in-law against her mother-in-law; and a man's foes will be those of his own household. He who loves father or mother more than me is not worthy of me; and he who loves*

son or daughter more than me is not worthy of me. . . . (Matt. 10: 35–37.)

This was a lesson he had to learn in order to undertake his ministry, leaving the gentle tyranny of Mary's love. And she also had to learn that she could no longer expect to occupy a special position in his life because of her ties of blood if she was to become a part of his new family in the faith. These years at the beginning of Christ's ministry must have been difficult for this couple. Mary had to accept her son's independence from her home, her control, and her ideas. But more than this, to become his mother again, she had to accept a reversal of their roles, admitting his leadership and subscribing to his ideas.

We know from the Scripture that she was modest enough, flexible enough, and faithful enough to do just this. She became in time one of the women who followed him, a faithful group including Mary, the mother of James, and Mary Magdalene. They eventually followed to the very foot of the cross, witnessing the crucifixion to its bitter end. The Pieta is the classic role for woman, holding the dead son on her knees as she had held the living baby to her bosom. So often the women are the followers and the mourners, those who bear the children, nurture them, release them, and finally mourn them. Whether such a scene actually occurred is not recorded, but we do see Mary with the other women performing the traditional woman's duties. They went to the tomb to see that everything was done properly and then they returned to prepare spices and ointments. The mourning process for women is partly the lamentation, partly the sharing of pain with the community of mourners, partly the adaptation of life to new dependencies and concerns, but largely mourning is worked out through the housewifely rituals which keep the hands busy and the mind organized. Mary here echoes Martha and Mary at the death of Lazarus—and all those women throughout the ages who have lost their greatest human treasure. The saddest of deaths is the early death of a child: to have spent so much love, nourished such hopes, watched the development of such potential, and then to have seen it all destroyed in a moment. The young should by all rights hold the aged parents in their arms, watching them die after long lives. In this natural order of things, the old find hope in the future of their children, the young find comfort in the past of their parents. But the loss of one's beloved son in the fullness of his maturity is the real test of faith. For the widowed Mary, it might have been her darkest moment—except for her memories of his words about life everlasting and the coming of the Comforter.

Mary's career did not end with the death of her son. She had the thrilling knowledge of his resurrection and heard the frequent reports of his appearance to those who knew him. She joined with the other women and men who had been loyal to him, following him from Galilee to Jerusalem. Her other sons now joined her in her conviction of Jesus' blessedness, and they all stayed in the crowded city, praying constantly in the Upper Room. By now, Mary had truly learned that this cluster of followers and believers was the real family of Jesus.

This Mary came to be one of that select group who heard the sound from heaven "like the rush of a mighty wind" and saw "tongues as of fire" and felt herself filled with the Holy Spirit. Speaking in tongues, full of their joy in the coming of the Spirit, these first Pentecostals seemed drunken in their prophetic utterances.

Scripture does not record the end of Mary's life, not because it dragged on in weary drudgery like Eve's, but because it had no end. Having accepted the real transcendence of her son, having admitted that family is more than blood-ties, having found that the child may lead the parent, she also discovered the indwelling of the Holy Spirit and the inconsequence of death. Her resurrected son awaited her as she lived out those last years of service on earth. Death for the Christian is a release from the cloudy, limited, incomplete life on earth. Mary awaited death sure in the knowledge that she would see her son and her Redeemer. It must have warmed her heart to see another of her sons becoming one of the leaders of the early church.

It is not surprising that Mary should have become such a significant symbol to much of Christendom. Though Jesus never placed her blessedness above the others of his "family" of saints, she does bear special ties with him and with us that are enormously moving. Mary, does, in fact, summarize most of the roles and experiences of women, and in doing so, redeems the image of Eve:

> When faced with free choice, she chose to abase her will to the will of God. She lived for and through her son, yet learned a lesson that transcended simple blood ties. She nurtured him and then released him, choosing to become his disciple rather than striving to manipulate him and plan his life.

Though concerned about the physical care of her family, she was more concerned with learning the truth her itinerant son preached, even to the point of leaving home to follow him.

Though poor and widowed, she learned that a new life is available to those who will believe. Though witness to her son's death, she discovered that death is no longer the victor.

Mary's story is both history and legend. Unlike the usual biography, this narrative does not include many typical details: her birth, her death, the births of her other children, the death of Joseph, etc. Instead, she is ancillary to her son. We know nothing of her that does not bear on him and his church. The history was undoubtedly transmitted orally among the early disciples and apostles. Stories that Mary had long cherished quietly in her heart could now be shared with others who knew the wonder of her son. As a mother she had more memories than these recorded, but not all such memories touch other lives in a significant way. Others would have no interest, for example, in his work at the shop, his favorite foods, his pets or toys or childhood friends—though we are hungry to know more such minutiae. Apocryphal writings include among them many half-remembered stories of childish incidents that the early church fathers believed inconsistent, erroneous, or from doubtful and uninspired sources.

Thus time, memory, interest, and scholarship gradually winnowed out the story of Mary, leaving us a few brief pages and a handful of quotes. The Scripture picks out those high points: the annunciation, the preparation, the birth, the flight, the scene at the Temple, the marriage at Cana, the renunciation, the crucifixion, and Pentecost. This is a record of a journey from youth to age, from madonna to pieta, from the call to the redemption.

The larger archetypal pattern of the heroic journey from birth to apotheosis (which is the male myth, not the female) has been supplied by popular tales. Easily replacing female deities of the Greek and Roman pantheon, Mary often assumed features of Athena or Diana or Aphrodite as the people chose to picture her. By the high middle ages, this simple Hebrew woman was celebrated as a great philosopher, versed in all branches of learning. Artists transferred the Aphrodite-Cupid imagery to madonnas, which in time grew increasingly stylish and sensuous. Dissatisfied with the dearth of information, the folk, the clergy, and the artists gradually developed a much fuller narrative of her mysterious birth, her youth and betrothal, and her assumption. The meagre details of Scripture (Matthew, for instance, barely mentions her) left humans with a hunger for a fully developed, compassionate motherly goddess.

It was thus the human embroidery of Scripture that made Mary into Our Lady, the Sophia figure who provides man with a comforting mother, an inspiration, an idea. It is to such a figure that Dante aspires; her love and the love of his earthly lady, who is her image on earth, draw him up toward Heaven. This particular role of woman, to stand on a pedestal and inspire men to live better lives, to seek higher ideals, has no real basis in Scripture, and certainly not in Mary, the blessed mother.

The Mary of Scripture stands crisply outlined as a real woman, a Jewess and a mother. She needs no elaborate history, no throne, no blue and golden robes. In the understatement of her poetic responses to God and the realistic reactions to her son we see the lineaments of a beautiful human being. We know that Jesus, in spite of his love for her, found her wrong in at least three recorded events: at the Temple, at the marriage at Cana, and at the house in Galilee. In all of these cases, she tried to draw him down to her human concerns; and he had to remind her of his higher calling.

Scripture often records, as noted before, only the typical, the miraculous, or the significant events. It characterizes Mary through her words and actions, not through elaborate description. The reader must bring his own experience to her portrait to test the truth of her portrayal. Her role of mother bears up well under such a test, for in Mary we recognize the irritating, bossy, hovering woman as well as the loving, loyal, and courageous disciple. She was fully human, but a suitable vessel for the seed of God.

Mary was neither so perfect as Christ nor so sinful as Eve. Though willing to accept her blessedness at the annunciation, she was reluctant to recognize her son as Christ; apparently she was slower than several of the disciples and other followers. She did know during the pregnancy and the early youth of Christ that he was God's Son. Her own training in Judaism must have prepared her for what this meant. But no one could fully prepare a woman for the day-to-day adjustment to living with the Messiah. She must have weighed her great honor and his great destiny against the comfortable contentment of normal people. Even Elizabeth could not share her experience fully.

In some ways, Mary seems to have been a "Jewish Mother," hovering over her miraculous child. We suspect too that, if Mary had had her own way, Jesus would have spent a long life in the carpenter shop, married to a nice Nazarene girl, a comfort to his aging mother and a respectable member of his community. Mary's will was only occasionally at one with God's will, but she did learn to subordinate her will to his.

Because of her humanity, Mary became a beautiful symbol of redeemed woman. She, like Eve, had the freedom to choose, and she chose well. She found blessedness in the pain of childbirth, she found joy in the subordination of self. And she finally became a helper in the community of believers, no longer demanding ties of the flesh. While Eve found that her sin bore bitter fruit, Mary found that her love bore spiritual riches. Certainly she is a symbol of motherhood, but even more she is a symbol of God's use of woman (or any human) as an instrument of his will. Through her, his Word became flesh and dwelt among us. She is not our salvation or the means to it, but a sign of how God works through us when we submit to his will. In her we see that motherhood can be a blessed path, a sharing with God in the work of creation. In her growth and transformation, we see how God uses our pain to help us mature. With her we learn the true meaning of blessedness.

The children of the mother in Proverbs rose up and called her blessed. Elizabeth looked at the pregnant Mary and called her blessed too. And in the Sermon on the Mount, Jesus taught that true blessedness comes from poverty of spirit, mercy, peacemaking, and suffering for his sake. The Spirit and its fruits bring the real joy to woman. Mary found as a young woman that God saw her as a suitable vessel for his Son. He knew her as an old woman to be a suitable dwelling for his Spirit. Usually, in looking at Mary, we are inclined to say that the greatest blessedness woman could know is to be mother to such a Son. But the last image of Mary is happier than the first: Full of wisdom, ripe with experience, this mature woman finds her completeness in becoming the disciple to such a Savior.

Biblical Notes

1. Luke 1:28–38   4. Luke 2:40–52
2. Luke 1:46–55   5. Matthew 12:48
3. Luke 2:19

CHAPTER VII

Harlot, Mother, and Bride: Images of Revelation

Various of the prophets and kings have used feminine imagery in expressing symbolically what they recognized to be God's will. God himself was often described as a helpmeet in the same way Eve was introduced. His love was compared to the love of a woman for her children. Given the close ties between Jesus and his mother, his sensitivity to women, their worries, their needs, and their activities, it is not surprising that Jesus continued this use of feminine imagery. He compared God to a woman seeking her lost coin, and his contemporaries to the foolish virgins who made no preparation for the wedding. Among his loveliest images is that of the Bride—his church. He pointed to the disciples at one point and said that they were his mother and brothers. Harking back to the creation of man as male and female, Christ saw something of each in all of us. He did not need to focus on the clear delineation of roles, the strong differentiation of sexes, because he was concerned for the soul. Because of him, Paul looked around and called both men and women "sons of God."

Jesus combined a remarkable symbolic and spiritual vision of the kingdom with a remarkable realism about the activities and needs of the physical world. He could enrich even the commonest bit of human experience, enjoying it for itself and endowing it with deeper meanings.

His descriptions of spinning and weaving, for instance, sharply contrasted with the effortless beauty of nature, symbolized in the specific detail of the lilies of the field. He could and can break through the scurrying preparations of a Martha to a larger vision of the two real choices we make for life. Aware of details, the diminishing supply of wine or the problems of storing new wine in old skins, he turned these concerns of everyday life into symbols of larger values. Not food (which goes into a man's mouth) but words (which come out) are the real basis for judging his worth. In his homey but transcendent vision, Christ truly changed and continues to change the water of life into intoxicating wine.

This symbolic vision tends to disturb many Protestants, who have traditionally been more reluctant than Catholics to accept truth on any level other than on the dead level of facts. (Fiction was for centuries considered lying, in the blunt judgment of Puritans.) Parables, such as those that Jesus used, and the more extended allegories (such as *Pilgrim's Progress*) were reluctantly accepted by early Puritans, only because their spiritual values justified their fancifulness. But the preference lay in the unadorned, simple, factual truth. This has been less so for the Jew. Certainly many of the prophecies were not presented as literal truth. They live in the realm of poetry, which touches on the deeper responses of the imagination and emotions without any literal equivalent. Sometimes, as in Nathan's symbolic presentation of the lamb story to David, the fiction is a simplified means for dealing with the ethical situation at hand. In Isaiah's portrayal of a savior and a holy Jerusalem, the Jews had no literal equivalent to consider. They were forced to let the hope and truth of his beautiful vision rest in their hearts until their fulfillment should finally come—perhaps not for centuries.

In moving beyond the factual level, the author may make his stories more universal, less limited through specificities of time and place. Even the apparently specific parables of Jesus adopt this universalizing technique: He speaks of the problems of shepherds and the habits of sheep with knowledge, but without naming the shepherd or providing the location or the date of the event. In dealing with an experience this common to Hebrew experience, he makes it possible to locate it in any of hundreds of places in any of hundreds of years. The meaning lies in the shepherd's response to the lost sheep, not in the historical accuracy of the event.

The more we read, the more we realize (as we noted before) that the words (even the words of Scripture) are not the truth themselves, but the means by which we are inspired and allowed to find the truth. Jesus knew that his words, like good seed, might often fall on barren ground. *He who has ears to hear, let him hear,* he said over and over. He knew that the word without the receptive heart was not enough. Even the Pharisees heard the words, but so selectively that they used them only to search out heresies and veiled attacks on themselves. To the heart hardened against the Word, no words will suffice. The truth of Scripture comes to us through the miraculous intervention of those clumsy symbols for sound and thought that we call *words.* These symbols, often fragments drawn from a vast array of statements, devoid of tone of voice, gesture, or facial expression, often ripped from context, are the means by which the receptive and inquiring mind seeks to understand his God. The erroneous transcriptions, clumsy translations, and truncated passages damage even more our responses, which are limited by our own prejudices and ignorance. What a miracle that the Holy Spirit can guide us to an understanding of the ineffable through such awkward means! God was not only the original author and preserver of this great book, he wrote the history and created the characters —and he continues to write his book through our lives.

The more we read and study, the more we find in Scripture. This is true of any really good book: the better the book, the more value we discover in the rereading. The real danger in our response to Scripture lies in believing that we need to fear using our whole minds and all our knowledge in our study. Too often we limit God, the author, to a shallow, impotent, mirror of our own inadequacies. Certainly the God who created us and who preserved the Scripture through us and for us is capable of handling our little problems. He created us as symbol-makers; obviously he is capable of providing symbols that will speak to us. He works, as we have already seen, with literal events, with symbolic events, with poetry, with prophecy, with heroic tales, and with psychological drama. No form of communication and no range of human activities are beyond his power. We are limited in our interpretation of Scripture by our own ignorance of his greater wisdom and power, and we shall never have found every meaning hidden in these words until that final day. Like Miriam we have cloudy messages, but seek Moses' ultimate speech with God, which like Adam's, was face to face.

The great book of Revelation must be approached with such admonitions, for it is a book of mysteries and of symbols, pointing to the contemporary historical events, to the great visions of its writer, and to the future of mankind. It is also a book of summary, bringing together in its magnificent symbols the images we have perceived in specific women all through Scripture. John draws heavily on the apocalyptic visions of Daniel, the wide-ranging symbolism of the prophets. The language of symbolism builds through many examples over a long period of time or else it communicates nothing. God spoke to John through figures of Hebrew and Roman history, images from the life of Christ, experiences of the early church, and haunting events or monuments from the cities John knew. The grandeur of this book lies in its meaning, its wide range, its universal vision, and its beautiful symbols. Here is a clear example of a work which may be understood only partially in factual and historical detail. Its greater message lies in its archetypes, several of which are female archetypes.

We have already seen that the Hebrews had generally come to understand women through the roles they perceived them to play, roles which were relative to men: as wife, mother, sister, friend, temptress, or sovereign. In other cultures, women had similar portrayals. The mother could be earth mother (a creative force, even the original power in many people's beliefs) or a terrible mother (a destructive force which became the monster faced by the hero).* The wife could be the faithful, long-suffering Penelope type or the fiercely competitive Clytemnestra. The beautiful maiden could become either the goddess of wisdom or a seductive and ensnaring fertility goddess. Thus, pagan witches, sirens, and monsters are all variants of the same archetypes that the Israelites also developed.

In Revelation we see a brilliant extraction of those archetypes which spoke most powerfully to the Judeo-Christian world and which therefore summarize for us the meanings our culture and our faith have come to vest in the female image.

The Old Testament had consistently presented women not only as literal actors in the drama of God's world, but as symbols as well. We have already seen that Eve was earth mother and temptress, an explana-

*In The Great Mother, Erich Neumann charts these images, using examples from a vast array of cultures.

tion for the origin of sin and a study of the results of sin. Mary continued the imagery into the New Testament, as the virgin mother, the vessel of God's seed and the instrument of his will. Jezebel and Hosea's harlot wife were symbols of alien sensuality and sacrilege. Potiphar's wife was the trap for the God-fearing man, the woman at the well a symbol of hope for redemption of sinners. The dancing Salome was the variant of the tempting snake. The weeping women at the tomb symbolized the old victory of death and the new victory over death.

Christ had followed prophetic tradition by imposing a symbolic vision on Hebrew history, and Paul continued this symbolic understanding. He interpreted the ancient events and characters as shadows, types, and foreshadowings of the Christian figures. The very familiarity of the writings made this possible, and the Hebrew love of the written word made it appropriate. Revelation draws on this same pattern, expanding the shadows into imposing symbols. If Christ was there even at the creation, if he was not only in the Word, but he *was* the Word, if God created mankind in his own image, and if he controls human history, then the concept of types makes sense. The words, objects, events, and people all speak to a deep level of our understanding, for God's (and Christ's) image is within us all. Humanity was able to recognize and respond to Christ because they knew by history and instinct what Christ would be and how he would appear. The long schooling of the Jews should have made them the most fertile ground for responding to the incarnation of the Word, but Gentiles proved to be even more open. (Their Apollo and Dionysus, their rites of baptism and sacrifice led them to see in Christ the complete figure and life that they sought in their faint shadows.) Like the philosopher of Plato's cave myth, they could see their blood sacrifices, their substitutionary atonements, the resurrection from the dead as shadows cast by human fires, not the full light of day. In Christ, these people could find a fuller shape and a deeper meaning for those forms which had invariably drawn from them a deep response.

The symbolic patterns in Revelation therefore speak to an accepted Hebraic-Christian tradition and practice as well as echoing some pagan rites. The visions of the prophets had invariably incorporated symbols, because only symbols are the natural language of the ineffable experience, of the mystic moment. Most of the images of fire, animals, lampstands, clothing, etc., which John uses had appeared in Isaiah or Ezekiel or Daniel or in the Gospels. Of course, the symbolic pattern, like the parables, limited the understanding of the public, excluding the uninitiated and unbelieving, speaking as it did in disguised form to the initiated and receptive believers.

What makes it especially valuable for the critic exploring a theme in Scripture is that such symbolic expressions draw heavily on the collective experience and demonstrate more clearly than history what were the accepted views. For example, though history chronicles the rare cases of woman as sovereign, as warrior, as spinster, as friend, they are apparently either not deeply imbedded as archetypes in the human psyche, or they are not a part of the historical perception of woman's role among this group of people. (Actually, some of them do recur as symbols in other cultures.) They are therefore quite naturally omitted among the gallery of portraits in Revelation, which focuses on the more deeply felt traditions. Therefore, Revelation explores woman as Harlot, as Mother, and as Bride—those archetypes most common in the Judeo-Christian tradition.

The great Harlot—*Babylon the great, mother of harlots and of earth's abominations*—a woman *drunk with the blood of the saints and the blood of the martyrs of Jesus,* [1] appears first. She is introduced in the admonition to Thyatira, a city which tolerated *the woman Jezebel, who calls herself a prophetess and is teaching and beguiling my servants to practice immorality and to eat food sacrificed to idols.* [2] The old queen has scarcely changed through the centuries. She still hearkens to other gods and lures God's people to them. (The sin of idolatry, as noted previously, is the classic explanation of harlotry for the Jew.) How often the temptress had been the foreign woman, the temple prostitute, whose sensuality turned man from the God of Spirit to the gods of the flesh.

As in the case of the old pagan queen, so this one will be damned along with all who succumb to her temptations. *I gave her time to repent,* says God through John, *but she refuses to repent of her immorality. Behold, I will throw her on a sickbed, and those who commit adultery with her I will throw into great tribulation, unless they repent of her doings; and I will strike her children dead.* [3]

For the early Christian, the lures of paganism were somewhat different from those in the days of the prophets. But Astarte or Aphrodite, the mysteries of Baal or the mysteries of Dionysus are all perversions of God's clear message. Those who would be the brides of Christ often become instead harlots of Venus. Christian love feasts were turned into sensual orgies of gluttony and lust. Like the woman who abuses the treasure of her femininity, the church abused the treasure of its nature. The temple of the spirit — whether the human body or the house of God —became the scene of gross abuse. Therein is God outraged, and as Paul has said, God is not mocked.

Later, in the book, the Harlot returns as the contrasting symbol to the Mother; the angel cries out of her downfall, *Fallen, fallen is Babylon the great! . . . For all nations have drunk the wine of her impure passions.* [4] The book often equates cities with women. Here the wicked Babylon, the new Rome, is the female personification of pagan practices. Her perversion of religion appears in her abuse of the wine—the drink of intoxicating life, the symbol of Cana and of the Last Supper—which now becomes the drink of the gluttonous and the lustful. The emperor worship demanded by the Romans, like the practices required by the Babylonians, made mockery of true faith.

She again, following the path of Jezebel, found her destiny was death. The seventh angel poured his bowl into the air, resulting in a great earthquake. *The great city was split into three parts, . . . and God remembered great Babylon, to make her drain the cup of the fury of his wrath.* [5] Lives and cities built on sensuality will fall before the wrath of God.

The image is most fully explored later in Revelation: a *great harlot who is seated upon many waters, with whom the kings of the earth have committed fornication, and with the wine of whose fornication the dwellers on earth have become drunk.* [6] Her sumptuous life tempts men, like the prostitute of Proverbs, to come to her luxurious adulterous sheets and share her passions. She becomes a symbol of power perverted for selfish reasons, an image of flesh turned soft, of life lived for gratification of the flesh. Certainly wealth and power can corrupt, causing people to forget the stern and self-denying path of salvation. Splendor and luxury have a very real appeal to humanity, and in advanced civilizations are surely the fruits wily Satan uses for our temptation.

John, carried by the Spirit into the wilderness, saw her *sitting on a scarlet beast which was full of blasphemous names,* a woman *arrayed in purple and scarlet, and bedecked with gold and jewels and pearls, holding in her hand a golden cup full of abominations and the impurities of her fornication.* We are given her sign and name—*on her forehead was written a name of mystery: "Babylon the great, mother of harlots and of earth's abominations."*[7] He equates the city with the Roman Empire, which sat on the hellish beast, but we all know that the lures of the city are more universal and diverse than Babylon's or Rome's. Sodom and Gomorrah, the fleshpots of Egypt, the regal harems of Solomon's Jerusalem all echo the lesson of Babel. Whenever men gather together to celebrate themselves, they produce evil that exceeds the sum of its parts. As we have seen from Eden on, man is capable of terrible evil when solitary, but where two or more gather without the guidance of God, they produce horrors and violence of every manner.

The female symbolism here is interesting, for the kings are male and so is the beast which bears the woman. Thus, the Harlot is no sovereign, no power in her own right. Like Jezebel, she derives her strength from Satan, her authority from the lawful king. She tempts men to greater evil rather than being the main actor herself. She remains a symbol of temptation, not of sovereignty.

The symbols clearly indicate Rome, the growing power of the worldly church, perverse religions—all equivalents for ancient Babylon and her worship of the fleshly goddess Astarte. The painted woman reminds us of all the other harlot-priestesses of Jehovah's epic female antagonist. The experience of Hosea with his wayward wife becomes for John a fresh commentary on God's beloved people; like the harlot-wife, they turn their backs on him to whore after foreign gods. Asherah becomes in this magnificent, archetypal symbol, the image of lust, of worship of the flesh, of the whoredom of the spirit. The image is female, but the experience is universal:

Her fall reminds us of the fate of Jezebel:

> *Fallen, fallen is Babylon the great!*
> *. . . Render to her as she herself has rendered,*
> *   and repay her double for her deeds;*
> *   Mix a double draught for her in the cup she mixed.*
> *As she glorified herself and played the wanton,*
> *   so give her a like measure of torment and mourning.*
> *Since in her heart she says, "A queen I sit,*
> *I am no widow, mourning I shall never see."*

As in the ironic history of Sisera's mother, such arrogance comes just before a fall. God will judge her at last:

> *So shall her plagues come in a single day,*
> *Pestilence and mourning and famine,*
>   *and she shall be burned with fire;*
> *for mighty is the Lord God who judges her.* [8]

This scene of her death is even more detailed than Jezebel's, for John points to all those who fall with her. Her sumptuousness has kept fleets afloat, catering to her appetite for

> *gold, silver, jewels and pearls, fine linen, purple, silk and scarlet,*
> *all kinds of scented wood, all articles of ivory, all articles of costly*
> *wood, bronze, iron and marble, cinnamon, spice, incense, myrrh,*
> *frankincense, wine, oil, fine flour and wheat, cattle and sheep,*
> *horses and chariots, and slaves, that is, human souls.* [9]

All this accumulation of human splendor and dainties sadly echoes the earlier studies. While food was a burdensome necessity to provide and the wife of Proverbs was admired for her productive life, we had a healthy pleasure in the details of food. When clothing was sparse, it was the mark of the industrious woman that she spun, wove, dyed and sewed for her family. But now luxury exceeds real need and people live not from their own industry but from the enslavement of others. Her wealth, not her work, marks her life. And her friend, the merchant, will fall with her when her economy collapses.

Her values have been material ones. While the merchants prospered, the saints and the prophets were slain, and they are finally vindicated in her fall. She is a completely earth-bound figure, a corruptor of the flesh and the will, used by the Anti-Christ, but too sensual to be more than a tool. In a civilization like ours that caters so extravagantly to the flesh in amusement industries, cosmetics, food, pornography, etc., the enthroned harlot must become a striking symbol and her fall an ominous forewarning.

The opposite female image of John's Revelation is the Mother. Foreshadowing the medieval iconography of Mary, John describes a woman who appeared in heaven as a great portent, *clothed with the sun, with the moon under her feet, and on her head a crown of twelve stars; she was with child and she cried out in her pangs of birth, in anguish for delivery.* [10] This Mother-image, in contrast to the richly robed Harlot who follows her, has symbolic clothing from God's creation—the sun, the moon, the stars—lights of his good world. While the scarlet woman gloried in her power and became the arch-enemy of Jehovah, this woman gloried in her child, who is the chosen of God: Her travail, causing her to cry out in the pangs of birth, in the anguish of delivery, was rewarded when *she brought forth a male child, one who is to rule all the nations with a rod of iron.* The child, threatened by the great red dragon (which parallels the monster the Harlot rides) was caught up to God and to his throne, and the woman fled into the wilderness, where she had a place prepared by God. Her enemy, the red dragon with seven heads and ten horns, is the monster Satan, the state or condition of man who threatened the child of God as did Herod and Pharaoh. Woman's vulnerability at birth and the child's helplessness, like all human frailty, were compensated for by God's all enveloping love. He protected the woman and the child as he protected Moses and Jesus and all the generations of his chosen people. The godly Mother is presented as the preserver of life, its renewing power, the source of restoration. Like Mary, she is the instrument by which God brings his child to the world. Not her actions, but the actions of that son will restore mankind. Like John the Baptist, she is not the Savior, but only the preparation for the Savior, who steps aside when the one comes after her who is greater than she.

The Mother imagery here is a beautiful summary of the creative but passive power of woman. She receives the seed, nurtures it, and bears it, but she is not the initiator of the creative action, nor has she control over the destiny of the child. Even when enthroned with the natural symbols of day and night, she cannot compare with the majesty of God or the Lamb. No elders nor scroll for her, her dominion is over nature alone, and even there, only its lights—stars, moon, and sun.

From this, and from the ancient equation of light and intellect, it is easy to see how Mary would have become Sophia, the goddess of wisdom, the ideal light leading men to attainment of their highest selves. But the scriptural context makes her enthronement inferior to the diety's and her survival dependent on his protection. She is no goddess, but a symbol of the human receiving and nurturing the Word of God in the wilderness of this world and in the hopes of the next. Nor is she the literal, historical Mary. Rather, she is a larger symbol of woman and of God's people.

The woman did not stay like Deborah to fight the dragon, but like

Mary, she fled into the wilderness, where she had a place prepared by God. Like Israel, her safety was in his hands, her nourishment at his pleasure. The terrain to which the Mother fled is the symbolic landscape of nightmare. Abandoning the home that provided her security and comfort, she fled to the wilderness without a place to lay her head. Following the path of the freed Israelites and the Christian pilgrim, she rejected the treasures that can be stolen or rusted or eaten by moth, preferring instead the treasures of the Kingdom. (For the Israelites finally used their gold for God's tabernacle, rejecting their golden calf.) Leaving the settled kingdoms and the cities where men and women pursue their feverish ways, she followed the path of the prophets and of Christ into the uncharted landscape of God's world. It is not the forest of confusion or the jungle of fear, but the wild place where one can be alone with God. Though for some it may become the desert of sterility, for the true believer, it is a place of sojourn and enrichment.

In the Mother symbol, the vulnerability and frailty of woman become symbolic of the vulnerability and frailty of humanity. The woman with the male child, fleeing into the wilderness reminds us of the loving and victimized Hagar. But she also expands to encompass that protective, nurturing strength of women who live primarily for their children. Accepting the mystery and miracle of birth as their moment of greatness, they see the newly created being as a part of their own destiny and as a part of God's design that transcends the individual. Childbearing and nurturing, the age-old female functions, take on transcendent significance. They become symbols of God's creative design for his chosen people and of his omnipresent protection of his elect. As the woman's most precious jewel is her child, so God's great love is mankind. The enfleshment of his only Son testifies to this. Though humans have found, like the woman, that their lives seem often to be flight and their homes a pathless wilderness, they can be assured of God's protective love nourishing those who keep his commandments and bear testimony to his Son.

The final female image of Revelation is the Bride. Nearing the conclusion of his magnificent vision, John announces with a jubilant echo of the multitudes who welcomed Christ's triumphal entry:

> *Hallelujah! For the Lord our God the Almighty reigns.*
> *Let us rejoice and exult and give him the glory,*

> *for the marriage of the Lamb has come,*
> *and his Bride has made herself ready. . . .*[11]

Rather than the traditional epithalamion which sings of the physical beauty of the Bride, this vision instead proclaims the joy of the marriage. The Bride makes herself ready, *clothed with fine linen, bright and pure,* but the simple clothing is quickly explained as a symbol of the righteous deeds of the saints. Her righteousness is granted her, and therefore deserves no praise.

Solomon sang his lovely song to celebrate the beauty of his beloved and his coming marriage and the pleasures of nature in the springtime —the joys of life and love and sexuality. His traditional marriage song, which finds parallels in the folk music and poetry of many countries, has frequently been interpreted in allegorical terms. This union of the king and his bride is seen as an image pointing forward to Christ's union with his church. Certainly it is the basis of the image in Revelation too, but the difference in the emphasis is impressive. No mention is made of the Bride's physical beauty or the Groom's desire. Instead, we have the gently understated picture of the Bride in her plain garments, deserving and receiving no praise. The praise is reserved for the Groom and for the excitement of the marriage. Revelation provides no opportunity for idolatry or subversion of the real values.

Not in the wilderness nor in Babylon, but in the holy city of Jerusalem, John finally sees "the Bride, the wife of the Lamb." In a welcome relief after the horrors of the Last Judgment, we see the holy city with its river of the water of life (not the waters of commerce that bring dainties to the doomed Harlot), and all its garden of delights.

Here John hears the words of invitation: *The Spirit and the Bride say, "Come."*[12] Then, carried away to a mountain, the traditional site of the mystic union with God, he has his vision of Jerusalem descending out of Heaven, the spiritual contrast to the blasted Babylon. This majestic, orderly, pure city of God is the home for Christ and his Bride, a splendid Eden. The tree of life is here, with the throne of God. And it is to this new paradise that "the Spirit and the Bride say, 'Come.' "

Like Christ to the woman at the well, they offer to *him who is thirsty . . . water of life without price.* Like the many maidens at the many wells, the Bride offers a warm welcome to the weary pilgrim. Reminding us of the wedding at Cana, where by the touch of Christ, the ordinary became the intoxicating, reminding us too of his words to the Samaritan woman, this beautiful image enriches the innumerable gestures of hospitality recorded in Scripture.

The Bride has traditionally been the image of beauty, of purity, of love—a reflection of Eve before the Fall. Her union echoes that first union of male and female—a re-union in fact, whereby in marriage the two again became one flesh. As that was a union of male and female, the Incarnation was a union of human and divine, and the redemption is a union of mankind with Christ. Jesus used the symbol, Paul expanded it, and John explained it.

While the female symbols of Revelation are still male-oriented, still built on woman's relationships with man, they really transcend male-female designations. The scarlet woman represents men and women who are citizens of Babylon; the Mother becomes all of God's chosen people; and the Bride is the whole church.

What greater tribute, in fact, could John pay to woman than to repeat Christ's own imagery of the Bride? And what a fitting contrast to Eve: to step into the garden of holy Jerusalem, to have yet another chance to eat of the tree of life, to be invited to reunite with God. The final invitation is one from male and female united, from Christ and his Bride, who say, "Come." In Revelation we see woman—and man—fully redeemed, fully restored to humanity, through Christ reborn in the image of God.

Biblical Notes

1. Revelation 17:5–6
2. Revelation 2:20
3. Revelation 2:21–23
4. Revelation 18:2–3
5. Revelation 16:19
6. Revelation 17:1–2
7. Revelation 17:3–5
8. Revelation 18:2, 6–8
9. Revelation 18:12–13
10. Revelation 12:1–5
11. Revelation 19:6–8
12. Revelation 22:17

Selected Bibliography

Anderson, Bernhard W. *Understanding the Old Testament.* Second Edition. Englewood Cliffs, N.J.: Prentice-Hall, 1966.

Beauvoir, Simone de. *The Second Sex.* Translated and edited by H. M. Parshley. New York: Bantam, 1970.

Buttrick, G.A., Commentary Editor. *The Interpreter's Bible,* Volume I. Nashville: Abingdon, 1956.

Chase, Mary Ellen. *Life and Language in the Old Testament.* New York: Norton, 1955.

Cole, William Graham. *Sex and Love in the Bible.* New York: Association, 1959.

Deen, Edith. *The Bible's Legacy for Womanhood.* Garden City, N.Y.: Doubleday, 1970.

Gehman, Henry Snyder, editor. *The New Westminster Dictionary of the Bible.* Philadelphia: Westminster, 1970.

Graves, Robert and Patai, Raphael. *Hebrew Myths: The Book of Genesis.* Garden City, N.Y.: Doubleday, 1964.

Neumann, Erich. *The Great Mother: An Analysis of the Archetype.* Translated by Ralph Manheim. New York: Pantheon, 1955.

Patai, Raphael. *The Hebrew Goddess.* New York: Ktav, 1967.

Reik, Theodor. *The Creation of Woman.* New York: Braziller, 1960.

———— *The Temptation.* New York: Braziller, 1961.

Wright, G. Ernest. *Biblical Archaeology.* Philadelphia: Westminster, 1957.